CIRCULAR WALKS
ON ANGLESEY

ISBN: 0-86381-478-6

Cover design: Alan Jones

Published by Gwasg Carreg Gwalch,
12 Iard yr Orsaf, Llanrwst, Wales LL26 0EH
☎ (01492) 642031
Printed and published in Wales.

Circular Walks
on Anglesey

DOROTHY HAMILTON

GWASG Carreg Gwalch

Contents

The Walks

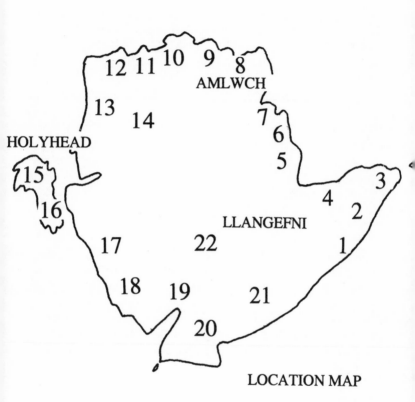

LOCATION MAP

Introduction

The walks in this guide to Anglesey are 2-8 miles long. They have been chosen for their outstanding, varied scenery and historical interest. Routes that are rewarding for naturalists are included.

All the walks have easy to follow directions and sketch maps. The starting points are at or near a car park or parking place. Directions are given to reach the start by car and – where possible – by public transport. Bus timetables are available from Tourist Information Centres.

The routes are graded according to length and terrain. Easy walks are short, all under 5 miles, with gentle, uphill sections. Moderate walks start at 4.5 miles and have more variation in landscape. Some of the walks classed as strenuous reach the highest points on the island and, although these are low hills compared to mountains, a few paths may be rough or steep in places. The average length of time taken to complete each walk is given. All routes are on Landranger 1:50 000 Sheet 114. Pathfinder maps 1:25 000 give greater detail and the appropriate map number is given for each walk. Points of interest give background information relating to the landscape and historic sites in each area. Facilities list alternative parking, toilets, pubs, cafes and places to visit.

In hot weather it is advisable to carry drinks on the longer walks – cafes and pubs are sparse in some places. Take adequate clothing and wear stout shoes or boots. Finally, avoid cliff paths in high winds and, at all times, take care.

Background

Anglesey is separated from the mainland of north-west Wales by the Menai Strait. Although an island, it is geologically part of a coastal plain which sweeps north and west from the mountains of Snowdonia. The gentle, undulating interior is skirted by a varied, mainly unspoilt, rugged coastline of spectacular cliffs, sandy beaches and remote coves. Offshore lie innumerable, small islands. From its isolated hills such as Mynydd y Garn, Mynydd Bodafon and Mynydd Eilian there are extensive views over Anglesey and south to the mainland while, on exceptionally clear days, the panorama extends to the mountains of Ireland and the Lake District. Anglesey has one of the driest climates in Wales – when Snowdonia is shrouded in mist and rain, the island is often bathed in sunshine. Almost all the coastline is a designated Area of Outstanding Natural Beauty.

The diverse habitats of Anglesey have a great deal to offer the naturalist. On the high cliffs of South Stack, Holy Island (Ynys Gybi), thousands of seabirds nest under the protection of the RSPB. The rare chough may be seen here and on the north-west coast. Another reserve is at Cemlyn where, behind a shingle ridge, four species of tern breed on islands in a brackish lagoon. A lesser known, inland nature reserve is Cors Goch, near Benllech. This calcareous fen, with its surrounding grassland and heath, supports a remarkable variety of plant and insect life. On the eastern side of the island, the limestone cliffs are covered with flowers in spring and early summer. Black guillemot breed on National Trust land at Fedw Fawr. The National Nature Reserve of Newborough Warren is an extensive area of dunes, renowned for its numerous plants. Part of the dunes have been planted with Corsican pine and, beyond the forest, the Cefni Estuary and Malltraeth Pool attract wading birds. A number of lakes, including Llyn Alaw, Llyn Cefni, Llyn Coron and Llyn Maelog, are recommended bird watching sites.

Anglesey became an island at the end of the last Ice Age when retreating glaciers melted and flooded and deep valley that became the Menai Strait. The bedrock of the island is Pre-Cambrian, a very ancient rock, which is visible in the dramatic cliffs at South Stack. It forms the rugged hill of Mynydd Bodafon. Covering this underlying rock are blankets of younger shale, as on Parys Mountain, while deposits of limestone are evident on the eastern side of the island at Penmon, Fedw Fawr and Bwrdd Arthur. Melting glaciers deposited a thick covering of glacial drift and boulder clay which has given Anglesey its rich fertile soil, ideal farming country. Agents of erosion have left a series of shallow valleys running north-east to south-west, of which a good example is Malltraeth Marsh.

Anglesey's position in the Irish Sea and its fertile soils have attracted settlers from prehistoric times. At Aberffraw, the excavation of a headland site revealed a vast quantity of flints from the Mesolithic era, around 6000 BC. The island, then, was still joined to the mainland; the sea, although still rising from the melting of the icecap had not yet flooded the valley which forms the Menai Strait. This took place about 1000 years later, when the sea almost divided Anglesey in two between Malltraeth and Red Wharf Bay. At that time, Holy Island (Ynys Gybi) became a separate island. The people of the Mesolithic (Middle Stone Age) era were hunters and one of the most important changes in human history followed them when new societies settled down to practise agriculture. These Neolithic (New Stone Age) people who arrived in Anglesey about 3500 BC were the first farmers. They cleared woodland for their fields and built stone tombs for their dead. Several tombs remain on the island and four are visited on the walks – Pant y Saer, Lligwy, Barclodiad y Gawres and Bodowyr.

Towards the end of the Neolithic era, Beaker pottery appeared on Anglesey. Pieces of this distinctive pottery have been found on Newborough Warren, Castell Bryn Gwyn, Lligwy and other sites. The next phase of culture was the Bronze Age, which was marked by the introduction of metal working. Copper was mined on Parys Mountain about 1600 BC. Round barrows, standing stones and stone circles are monuments that remain from this period. Anglesey does not have any surviving stone circles although the two huge standing stones at Castell Bryn Gwyn may be the remains of one.

Celtic tribes from Central Europe moved into Britain during the 6th century, the commencement of the period known as the Iron Age. Substantial farmsteads and round huts were built. Iron replaced bronze and pottery was scarcely used. Hillforts were established on promontories and hills as protection against invasion. Walks visit the superb hillforts of Bwrdd Arthur, Dinas Gynfor and Caer y Twr. The hut groups of Din Lligwy and Ty Mawr continued to be occupied during the Roman occupation. Caer Leb and Castell Bryn Gwyn, Brynsiencyn, belong to this period although the latter was first constructed in Neolithic times. Amazing Celtic offerings were found in a sacred lake, Llyn Cerrig Bach, during the 2nd World War when a runway was being built at RAF Valley. The artefacts were mainly

9

military objects, such as spears, swords, chariot wheels, harnesses and chains. They dated from about 200 BC to AD 60 and are thought to be goods captured in war. They were thrown into the lake as offerings to gods. At the time of the Roman invasion, Anglesey was the major centre for the Druids. The Roman leader, Suetonius Paulinus, was determined to put an end to the old religion when he crossed the Menai Strait in AD 61 with an army of more than 10,000. In one devastating battle, the Romans slaughtered the Druidic priests and destroyed the sacred oak groves, thus wiping out the Celtic religion. Paulinus left Anglesey to suppress a revolt in the south-east led by Queen Boudicca and it was AD 78 before the Romans re-crossed the Strait again, this time led by Agricola. Anglesey was then ruled from the Roman fort Segontium at Caernarfon and a fort and naval base were established at Caergybi *(Holyhead)*. The remains of a Roman signal station can be seen on Holyhead Mountain.

About the time the Romans left Wales, Celts from Northern England came south to help fight and expel the Irish who were invading Anglesey and North Wales. Later, a royal court was founded at Aberffraw and the church at nearby Llangadwaladr was the kings' burial ground. During the 5th and 6th centuries Christian missionaries reached Anglesey founding churches and monasteries. The Christian ruler, Maelgwn Gwynedd, provided land for monasteries at Holyhead and Penmon. Reminders of the saints' presence are the holy wells – St Seiriol's at Penmon, St Gwenfaen's at Rhoscolyn and St Dwynwen's well on Llanddwyn Island. In the 9th century, Merfyn Frych (the Freckled) and Rhodri Mawr fought battles with the Viking raiders who crossed the Irish Sea from their bases at Dublin and the Isle of Man. At that time, the court at Aberffraw was a centre of culture where travelling scholars were shown hospitality. The Viking invasions persisted and in 968 the palace at Aberffraw was partly destroyed. The monasteries also came under attack in 961 and 967. The raiders failed to make any settlements and Viking names are the only evidence of their presence: Anglesey (island in the sea), Priestholm and Skerries.

A Norman invasion of Anglesey in 1090 by the Earl of Chester led to the building of a motte type castle at Aber Lleiniog (near Llangoed). Four years later it was captured by Gruffudd ap Cynan and, with the cessation of Viking raids, a prosperous period followed during which stone churches were built, replacing the earlier wooden structures. The abbey church at Penmon, Capel Lligwy (near Moelfre) and the unusual west tower of Llaneilian church are 12th century. At the same time, the interior of the island was finally cleared of its woodland, releasing the fertile soil for agriculture. In the Middle Ages huge quantities of grain were grown here and Anglesey became known as Môn Mam Cymru – Anglesey, Mother of Wales – meaning the supplier of food.

The power of the medieval Welsh Princes reached its peak during the reign of Llywelyn ap Iorwerth (the Great), titled Prince of Aberffraw and Lord of Snowdon. He constructed strategic castles at Dolbadarn, Cricieth, Berre and Dolwyddelan to guard his territory on the mainland. Abbeys and friaries were founded and his wife Siwan, Joan daughter of King John, was buried at the Franciscan friary at Llanfaes, near Beaumaris. The site of his court at Rhosyr (Newborough) has recently been excavated, revealing the foundations of a large hall. Some 15 years after Llywelyn's death, his grandson Llywelyn ap Gruffudd (later known as Llywelyn the Last) gained control over Gwynedd and in 1267 Henry III acknowledged his title Prince of Wales. When Henry died in 1272 he was succeeded by his son, Edward I, a king who would not tolerate opposition. Conflict between Llywelyn and Edward culminated in war 1276-7 and again in 1282. During these wars Edward seized the corn harvest from Anglesey to weaken the country's resistance. Whilst in Mid Wales, Llywelyn was killed. Dafydd, his brother, was captured and executed the following year. The death of Llywelyn brought an end to Welsh independence and Anglesey became a county in 1284. It was now the king's eldest son who received the title Prince of Wales. Edward consolidated his victory by a programme of castle building. In 1294, the partly built castle at Caernarfon was stormed during a revolt under Madog ap Llywelyn. Work began on Beaumaris Castle in 1295, but it was never completely finished. It was captured by Owain Glyndwr's troops in 1403 and they held it for two years.

In 1485, Henry Tudor, the grandchild of an Anglesey man, defeated King Richard III at the Battle of Bosworth. He became Henry VII, the first Tudor Monarch. His grandfather, Owain Tudor, was born

11

at Plas Penmynydd, a farmhouse on Anglesey. It is off the B5420, not far from the Afon Ceint. Owain went to London as a young man to join Henry V's court. When Henry died he left a young widow, Catherine de Valois, daughter of the King of France, who fell in love with Owain, and they secretly married in 1429. The elder son of this union, Edmund, married Margaret Beaufort, but Edmund died shortly afterwards. However, his widow was pregnant and, at 14 years old, she gave birth to Henry Tudor, the future king.

During the 18th century the small fishing village of Amlwch grew into a boom town of 6000. Over 1000 people worked the copper veins on Parys Mountain. At its peak, the mine was producing over 40,000 tons of ore each year, mainly for the European navies. The harbour was enlarged to berth ore carrying ships and it became a thriving port. Another industry on Anglesey was limestone, most of which was quarried on the eastern side of the island for local use and export. The stumps of old windmill towers seen scattered about the island are from the 18th and 19th centuries.

From the Middle Ages ferries transported people across the Menai Strait and by the 17th century many of these passengers continued on the packet boats to Ireland. The importance of Anglesey on this route was increasingly recognized and early in the 19th century Thomas Telford built his graceful suspension bridge across the strait. He also constructed the new coach road, the A5. Shortly afterwards, Robert Stephenson built the Britannia Bridge and by 1850 it was possible to travel by train from London to Holyhead. By this time, lighthouses were operating along the coast and the island's lifeboat service was in use. Anglesey's treacherous rocks, close to Liverpool's sea lane, were responsible for hundreds of shipwrecks.

Rail and road networks led to the development of tourism at small coastal resorts. Nowadays, apart from a small amount of modern industry, most of the island's interior remains dominated by agriculture.

Welsh Place-names

The following words are often used in place-names on Anglesey.

Many refer to geographical features or have historical connections.

Aber – *estuary, river mouth*
Adar – *birds*
Afon – *river*
Allt – *slope*
Arwydd – *signal*
Bach/Fach – *small*
Bedd – *grave*
Brith – *speckled*
Bryn – *hill*
Bwa – *arch*
Bwlch – *pass*
Cae – *field*
Caer – *fort*
Capel – *chapel*
Carn – *cairn*
Carreg – *rock*
Carw – *deer*
Castell – *castle*
Cefn – *ridge*
Celli/Gelli – *grove*
Coch – *red*
Coed – *wood*
Cors/Gors – *bog, marsh*
Craig – *rock*
Croes – *cross*
Cromlech – *burial chamber*
Cwm – *valley*
Dinas – *fort*
Dôl/Ddôl – *meadow*
Du/Ddu – *black*
Dwr – *water*
Dyffryn – *valley*
Eglwys – *church*
Ffordd – *road*
Ffynnon – *spring, well*

Garn – *cairn*
Glan – *river bank*
Glas – *blue, green*
Gwyn – *white*
Gwynt – *wind*
Hafod – *summer dwelling*
Hen – *old*
Hendre – *winter dwelling*
Hir – *long*
Isaf – *lower*
Llam – *leap*
Llan – *church*
Llyn – *lake*
Llys – *court, palace*
Maen – *stone*
Maes – *field*
Mawr/Fawr – *big, great, large*
Melin – *mill*
Moel/Foel – *bare, hill*
Morfa – *marsh*
Mynachdy – *monastery*
Mynydd – *mountain*
Nant – *stream*
Newydd – *new*
Ogof – *cave*
Pant – *hollow, valley*
Parc – *park, field*
Pen – *head, top*
Penrhyn – *promontory, headland*
Pentir – *headland*
Pentre – *village*
Plas – *mansion*
Pont – *bridge*
Porth – *port*
Pwll – *pool*

Rhiw – *hill*
Rhos – *moorland*
Rhyd – *ford*
Tafarn – *inn*
Traeth – *beach*
Tref – *town*
Trwyn – *promontory*

Twr – *tower*
Ty – *house*
Tyddyn – *small farm*
Uchaf – *upper*
Y/Yr – *the*
Ynys – *island*
Ysgubor – *barn*

Walk Reference Guide

The following lists are a quick guide to the different types of walks in this book and their historic interest. The walks in the natural history list visit reserves or other rewarding areas.

Coast Walks: 3, 4, 6-10, 12, 13, 15-18, 20
Hilltop Walks: 4, 7, 8, 13, 15
Woodland Walks: 20, 22
Lakeside Walks: 17, 19
Natural History Walks: 2, 3, 5, 10, 11, 15, 17, 19, 20

Stone Age Sites: 5, 6, 17, 18, 21
Bronze Age Sites: 14, 21
Iron Age Sites: 3-6, 10, 15, 21

Wells: 3, 8, 16, 20
Churches: 3, 6-8, 10, 12, 14, 16, 18-21
Medieval Court, Castles: 1, 2, 20
Industrial Heritage: 8-10, 14, 15

Information Centres

Holyhead Tourist Information Centre	01407 762622
Llanfairpwll Tourist Information Centre	01248 713177
Cemaes Information Centre	01407 710004
Llys Llywelyn Coastal Heritage Centre	01407 730797
Ellin's Tower Seabird Centre	01407 764973
Weathercall	0891 500415

Country Code

1. Guard against any risk of fire.
2. Keep to the public rights of way when crossing farmland.
3. Avoid causing any damage to walls, fences and hedges.
4. Leave farm gates as you find them.
5. Keep dogs under control and on leads in the presence of livestock.
6. Leave machinery, farm animals and crops alone.
7. Take care not to pollute water.
8. Carry your litter home with you.
9. Protect all wildlife, plants and trees.
10. Avoid making any unnecessary noise.
11. Drive carefully on country roads.
12. Enjoy and respect the countryside.

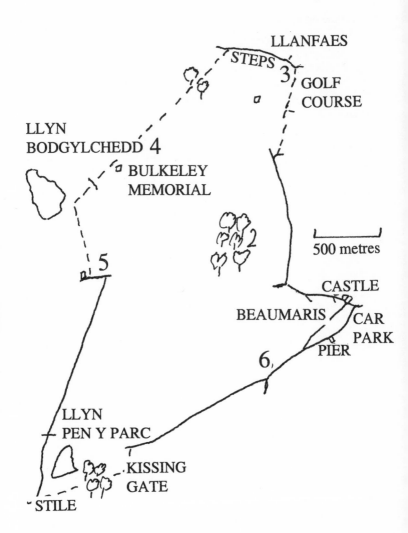

LLANFAES

STEPS 3

GOLF
COURSE

LLYN
BODGYLCHEDD 4

BULKELEY
MEMORIAL

2

500 metres

5

CASTLE

BEAUMARIS
CAR
PARK

PIER

6

LLYN
PEN Y PARC

KISSING
GATE

STILE

Beaumaris (Biwmares) – Llanfaes – Bulkeley Memorial – Llyn Pen-y-Parc – Menai Strait (Afon Menai) – Beaumaris (Biwmares)

OS Maps:	1:50 000 Landranger Sheet 114; 1:25 000 Pathfinder Sheets 751, 752.
Start:	Beaumaris Castle, G.R. 606762.
Access:	From Menai Bridge (Porthaethwy) town centre take the A545 to Beaumaris. Buses from Bangor.
Parking:	Large car park on The Green.
Grade:	Moderate – mostly field paths and lanes.
Time:	3 hours.

Points of Interest:

1. The town of Beaumaris dates from the building of the castle. Work commenced in 1295 for Edward I, the architect being the Savoyard, James of St George. The chosen site was an unoccupied marshy area – 'Beaumaris' originates from the Norman French words 'beau mareys' meaning 'fair marsh'. The levelness of the site helped to achieve the plan of a perfectly symmetrical, concentric design. A channel linked the moat surrounding the castle to the sea. However, money ran out and the structure was never completed. It lacks the high towers and battlements of fortresses such as Harlech and Conwy. This was the last of the castles built by Edward I to oppress the Welsh. Families from Llanfaes were evicted to Rhosyr, which became known as Newborough *(Niwbwrch)*. Meanwhile, having acquired its charter, the town of Beaumaris grew and prospered.

2. The now derelict Baron Hill mansion was the seat of the Williams-Bulkeley family. William Bulkeley came from Cheshire about 1440 when he was made Constable of the Castle. He married into an important local family and acquired much land. The tomb of William

Bulkeley and his wife Elen is in the Parish Church. They built a town house in Beaumaris, Henblas, which, regretably, was demolished in 1869. Later members of the Bulkeley family built the first Baron Hill mansion in 1618, and it was rebuilt in 1776 by Samuel Wyatt, a renowned architect. Further alterations were carried out about 150 years ago. In the 2nd World War it was a camp for the Royal Welch Fusiliers and a military hospital. Unoccupied since then, it is now a ruin and surrounded by trees. On his visit to Baron Hill, Pennant noted that the coffin of Siwan, Princess Joan, was in use as a horse watering trough. After being rescued, the coffin was displayed in a mausoleum in the grounds of Baron Hill. It is now in the porch of the Parish Church. The Bulkeley line passed to the Williams-Bulkeleys in 1822.

3. Formerly owned by the Hampton family, the building of Henllys Hall functioned as a monastery for 20 years before becoming a hotel in 1971. The medieval town of Llanfaes was probably situated where the modern village is now. Before Beaumaris was built, it was an important commercial centre and major port. No traces remain of the friary founded in 1237 by Llywelyn Fawr *(Llywelyn the Great)* in honour of his wife Siwan. The site is near the coast under fields and factory grounds. Siwan, Princess Joan, Llywelyn's wife and King John's illegitimate daughter, was buried at the Franciscan Friary, her body transported across the Lavan Sands *(Traeth Lafan)*. Other important ladies of Gwynedd were buried there, including Senena, Llywelyn's mother and Eleanor de Montfort, wife of Llywelyn ap Gruffudd. After the Dissolution of the Monasteries, during the reign of Henry VIII, the cover stone of Siwan's coffin was taken to Beaumaris Church.

4. The impressive Bulkeley Memorial, built of Penmon marble, was erected in 1876 in honour of a Sir Richard who died the previous year, aged 73. The history of the family has some dramatic events. In 1624, a Sir Richard Bulkeley died of suspected poisoning; there was evidence of arsenic or a similar poison in his tobacco. His widow soon married Thomas Cheadle who had worked for the family. However, the pair were not brought for trial until 1634. They were found Not Guilty because although there was strong evidence against them, it was not infallible. There was proof that poison was bought but not when

and the servant responsible for mixing the tobacco died before the date of the trial. Sir Richard left a son, another Sir Richard who wanted revenge.

5. The Almshouses were built in 1613. They were paid for through the will of David Hughes who also founded a free grammar school in the town. Red Hill, the hill south-east of here, was the site of a battle during the 2nd Civil War. The Royalist Constable, a Colonel Richard Bulkeley, lost the castle to Parliamentary forces in 1646. The islanders revolted and during the Battle of Beaumaris (1648) on Red Hill about 30-40 lives were lost on each side.

6. Before the building of the Menai Bridge in 1826 ferries transported people across the Strait. One of the earliest ferries went to Llanfaes, later it switched to The Green at Beaumaris. On the route for Ireland, Beaumaris became a post town and boats carried horses as well as people. The crossing of Lavan Sands *(Traeth Lafan)* was only safe in 3 or 4 hours out of every 12. Old charts show two routes – one passed below Penmaen Mawr, the other farther west. The Corporation paid for posts to be erected across the sands to guide people to the ferry. In later years the ferry terminal moved to Gallows Point then stopped altogether about 1830. It was on Lavan Sands that the Bulkeley-Cheadle feud came to an end. After the Civil Wars young Colonel Bulkeley travelled abroad. On his return, whilst on the sands, he met Richard Cheadle who had helped Parliamentary troops cross the Strait. They fought a duel and Bulkeley was slain. Cheadle was hanged at Conwy. About the time of the last ferries excursion boats from Liverpool started to call at Beaumaris. The Victorian pier was longer than it is now. La Marguerite, a paddle-steamer belonging to the Liverpool and North Wales Steamship Company, could carry over 2000 passengers.

Walk Directions: (-) denotes Point of Interest

1. From the castle entrance (1) take the road leaving the main street and pass the castle on your right. At the Catholic Church turn right along Rating Row to a road junction. Turn right past a pub, the Sailor's Return.

2. Take the lane signposted to Henllys Hotel (2). Pass Baron Hall East Lodge on the left.

3. At the driveway for the hotel bear right with the lane. In a few paces turn left on a footpath.

4. Follow the enclosed footpath until it emerges on a golf course. Keep ahead to a kissing-gate and lane (3).

5. Turn left and, in a short distance, left again uphill. Shortly after the lane starts to descend, go up steps on the left to a stile and footpath.

6. On reaching a field keep ahead by the left boundary to a small footbridge and ladder stile. Continue uphill to a bench – a good place for a break to enjoy the views.

7. Slant slightly right through bushes and trees to a stile. Keep ahead to the next stile. Head now towards the Bulkeley Memorial (4). Look back for fine views as far as the Great Orme at Llandudno. Before the monument climb a ladder stile and continue to the lane.

8. Cross the lane to another footpath. Follow the hedge on the right to the corner of the field and a view of Llyn Bodgylched. Turn left and descend the fields to a stile and lane by the Almshouses (5).

9. Turn left and take the next lane right. Cross over a crossroads and follow the winding lane past Llyn Pen-y-parc. Where the lane bends right, turn left over a stone stile.

10. Keep ahead, bearing slightly left downhill. Before a building on the right, swing left and go through a gap in the wall between a gatepost and gorse bush.

11. Take the path through the trees and bushes to a footpath signpost. Continue to a low post. At a fork take the left-hand path to a kissing-gate and field. Keep ahead to another kissing-gate and lane.

12. Turn right, downhill, to the road bordering the Menai Strait (6). Turn left into Beaumaris.

Facilities:

All facilities available in Beaumaris. Public toilets are at the start, near the castle. Camp site at Llanfaes. Many interesting buildings in the town including the Tudor Rose, a medieval hall-house. Boat trips from the pier.

Llangoed – Afon Lleiniog – Fedw Fawr – Mariandyrys – Llangoed

OS Maps:	1:50 000 Landranger Sheet 114; 1:25 000 Pathfinder Sheets 752, 735.
Start:	Car park at northern end of Llangoed village, G.R. 611797.
Access:	From Menai Bridge (Porthaethwy) town centre take the A545 to Beaumaris. Continue on the B5109 to Llangoed. Buses from Bangor and Menai Bridge.
Parking:	Car park at the northern end of Llangoed village before the bridge over the Afon Lleiniog.
Grade:	Moderate – paths, tracks and lanes.
Time:	3 hours.

Points of Interest:

1. A low motte, (Castell) Aber Lleiniog Castle, is on the opposite side of the river. During the Norman invasion the Earl of Chester built a timber castle on this man-made mound but it was soon captured by the Welsh under Gruffudd ap Cynan. In the 17th century Thomas Cheadle, who had married Richard Bulkeley's widow (see Beaumaris walk, point of interest 3), built a stone fort on the site. It became known as 'Lady Cheadle's Fort'. Thomas Cheadle turned traitor during the Civil War and offered the castle to Parliament. Royalists intercepted the letter and he was incarcerated in Beaumaris dungeon. Later, the fort was used by seamen from parliamentary ships in the Strait. The small, square castle, now a ruin, had a turret at each corner. To continue on the walk, return to the track.

2. This is Fedw Fawr, a 45 acre common owned by the National Trust, which is one of the few breeding sites for black guillemots. Fulmars, razorbills and gulls also nest on the limestone cliffs. There are

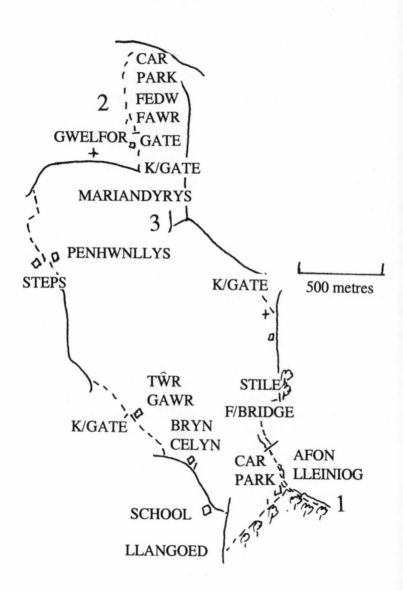

CAR
PARK
FEDW
FAWR

2

GWELFOR GATE
+

K/GATE

MARIANDYRYS

3

PENHWNLLYS

STEPS

K/GATE

500 metres

TŴR
GAWR

STILE

F/BRIDGE

K/GATE

BRYN
CELYN

CAR   AFON
PARK   LLEINIOG

SCHOOL

1

LLANGOED

22

extensive views along the coast and out to Puffin Island *(Ynys Seiriol)* and the Great Orme. Yellowhammers, stonechats, blackcaps and whitethroats may be seen or heard on the heath and scrubland. In summer the heath is colourful with flowers – bell heather, saw-wort, kidney vetch, mountain everlasting and various orchids.

3. From this point it is only a few minutes walk to the Mariandyrys Nature Reserve, which is cared for by the North Wales Wildlife Trust. The reserve is just 15 acres of common land, a hill of carboniferous limestone covered by heather, gorse and grassland. Linnets and dunnocks nest and the reserve is especially attractive to butterflies such as the grayling, brown argus, small tortoiseshell and painted lady. Plants include the common rockrose, burnet saxifrage and a number of orchids. To visit the reserve, turn right on the lane and at a T junction cross the stile to the left of the house opposite. A path climbs the hill, crossing a track, to an area of grassland from where there are fine views over the surrounding countryside. To continue on the walk, return to direction 9 and keep ahead on the lane.

Walk Directions: (-) denotes Point of Interest

1. Cross the little bridge over the Afon Lleiniog and immediately bear right. Turn right at a fork and follow the river until the track veers left to a gate. Keep ahead on the woodland path for about 150 metres (1).

2. Retrace your steps to the track. After a few more metres bear left on grass just before a house. Follow the left banking and continue on a path. At a junction of paths bear left to meet a road.

3. Turn right and in about 200 metres turn left on a road. Pass a school and ignore a lane on the right. Pass a house called Bryn Celyn and take the next lane right.

4. At the farm called Twr Gawr keep ahead and go through a kissing-gate. Continue by the left edge of fields until a kissing-gate gives access to a lane.

5. Turn right on the lane. When it bends left keep ahead on the track for Penhwnllys Plas. At the farm gate follow the new diversion up steps on the left and continue to a field. (If the diversion is not yet in

place go through the gate and cross the farmyard to the field.)

6. Keep ahead by the left edge of the field to a kissing-gate. Continue through similar gates, bearing right and then left on an enclosed path which leads to a lane.

7. Bear right and in 800 metres go through a kissing-gate on the left beside the drive for Gwelfor. Continue by the hedge on the right when the drive leaves it. Pass a house on the left and reach an enclosed path which leads to a gate. Take a path slanting left to join a wide path and follow it towards the sea (2).

8. After exploring Fedw Fawr take a path to the small car park and follow the narrow lane to a T junction (3).

9. Bear left to return to Llangoed. The lane goes past a few houses and rises between walls. Opposite a track on the left turn right through a kissing-gate.

10. The path descends through gorse and crosses an open field. Go uphill to have a cemetery on the right. Turn right on the lane.

11. Pass a school and continue another 500 metres to a stile on the right. Follow the left edge of the field and turn left over a footbridge to a kissing-gate.

12. Go past a cottage and follow the drive to a road. Turn right to the car park at the start.

Facilities:

Small car park at Fedw Fawr. Pub near end of walk.

Penmon Priory – Penmon Point (Trwyn Du) – Pentir – Penmon Priory

OS Maps:	1:50 000 Landranger Sheet 114; 1:25 000 Pathfinder Sheet 752.
Start:	Penmon Priory, G.R. 631807.
Access:	From Beaumaris take the B5109 north. In 1½ miles turn right at crossroads and right again at the next junction. Buses from Bangor and Beaumaris to crossroads 1¼ miles from the start.
Parking:	Small car park near the priory.
Grade:	Easy – mostly field paths and lane.
Time:	1½ hours.

Points of Interest:

1. St Seiriol founded a monastery here in the 6th century, during the reign of Maelgwn Gwynedd. The first church, a wooden structure, was destroyed by Vikings in the 10th century. Two centuries later the present church was built and the religious community eventually became an Augustian Priory. The ruined monastery comprises a refectory which had a dormitory above and a cellar below. Other buildings have gone but the prior's accommodation was converted into a house by the Bulkeleys of Beaumaris. The only remains from the early monastery are two crosses, and these are now inside the church. The tower, nave and transepts of Penmon Church are 12th century whilst the later chancel was entirely rebuilt in 1885.

2. This impressive dovecote was built around 1600 by Richard Bulkeley of Baron Hill, near Beaumaris. About 1000 pigeons were kept here, a source of food in the winter months. Eggs would have been collected from the nesting holes by placing a ladder on the

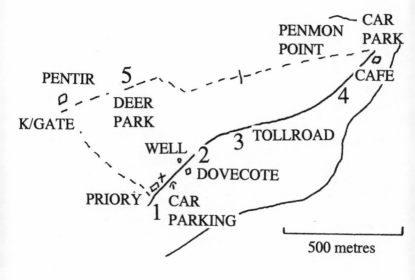

PENMON POINT

CAR PARK

PENTIR

5

DEER PARK

K/GATE

WELL

2

3 TOLLROAD

4

CAFE

DOVECOTE

PRIORY

1

CAR PARKING

500 metres

central pillar. Opposite the dovecote, across the road, a path goes past the monastic fishpond to St Seiriol's holy well. The spring, which emerges from the cliff, would have been a water supply for the monastery. The pool is surrounded by a brick structure that dates from about 1700, whilst the seating area may be from earlier times. It is thought that the saint lived nearby in a cell under the cliff. An old story is told of St Seiriol who used to walk across the island, once a week, to meet St Cybi who started from Holyhead. They met at the wells of Clorach, near Llannerch-y-medd. Because St Cybi was always facing the sun, travelling from west to east in the morning and east to west in the evening, he became suntanned and was called Cybi the Dark. St Seiriol, however, had the sun on his back on both journeys and remained pale. He became known as Seiriol the Fair.

3. On the right, between the road and the sea, lies the Flagstaff Quarry. About 100 years ago a cairn was found on the headland during quarrying operations. Inside the grave, which contained cremated bones, were two small pots known as accessory cups. They were characteristic of cups found in eastern England rather than Anglesey. Accessory cups are found in some graves of the Early Bronze Age. The stone used for building the Menai Bridge came from quarries at Penmon. Along the road there are superb views of Puffin Island and the North Wales Coast.

4. Puffin Island (Ynys Seiriol) is separated from Anglesey by a treacherous sound, 800 metres wide. St Seiriol built a sanctuary on the island in the 6th century and he is thought to be buried there. In AD 632, Cadwallon, King of Gwynedd, was besieged on the island by the Saxon king, Edwin of Northumbria. Whilst undergrowth conceals the ancient monastic cells, the 12th century 40 foot church tower is visible from above Penmon Point (Trwyn Du). Another disused building on the island is the 19th century semaphore station, one of a chain from Holyhead to Liverpool. The only inhabitants nowadays are gulls, cormorants, guillemots, puffins, rabbits and rats. At one time there was a trade in pickling puffins; their flesh was soaked in vinegar and spice before being packed in barrels and exported to England and France. Man and rats almost eliminated the puffin population.

The Penmon lifeboat station and lighthouse were built early in the 19th century, after the tragic sinking of the paddle-steamer, Rothsay Castle. This decrepit vessel was on a day trip from Liverpool to Beaumaris one day in August 1831. She was in such a worn out condition that several seamen refused to sail in her. Nevertheless, 150 passengers were aboard when she set out to sea in a strong north-westerly wind. After a few hours passengers asked the captain to turn about but he was already drunk and refused. It took 10 hours to reach the Great Orme and by the time they were near Puffin Island the ship needed bailing out, but there were no pumps or even buckets. The captain went overboard when the ship rammed into Dutchman's Bank. The funnel collapsed and smashed the ship's side, ripping it apart. Only 23 people survived. Penmon Point can be a good place for birdwatching if binoculars are carried. Cormorants, razorbills, fulmars, oystercatchers, gulls, terns and possibly puffins may be seen at sea. The heath and scrubland on Penmon Point are frequented by small birds such as stonechats, linnets and whitethroats. The flowers on this limestone headland include common rockrose and orchids. Various butterflies may be spotted on a sunny summer's day – orange-tip, small heath, peacock, clouded yellow, common blue and others.

5. This is one of the many hut circles to be found close to or in the deer park. They are thought to date from Early rather than Late Iron Age because of the lack of defensive structures. The wall of the deer park was built after the Dissolution of the Monasteries when the land came into the hands of the Bulkeley family. No deer have roamed the park since about 1914.

Walk Directions: (-) denotes Point of Interest

1. Starting from the priory (1) walk in the direction of the dovecote and St Seiriol's well (2).

2. Follow the toll road (3) to its end at Penmon Point *(Trwyn Du)* with fine views across the sound to Puffin Island (4).

3. Opposite the cafe take a wide path up to a marker post. From here a clear path continues up the hill to a ladder stile and field.

4. Keep ahead to another stile. Turn right on the track and before a gate go left over a stile.

5. Continue ahead by the right boundary of this field. Just before a gate cross a stone stile on the right. Follow the high deer park wall on the left to the next stile.

6. Continue with the wall on the left, passing a hut circle (5) close to the wall. At a white cottage turn left through a kissing-gate in the wall.

7. Bear half left and descend the hill diagonally to reach a fence on the right. Follow it to a stile. Continue downhill and on reaching the priory wall bear right to steps and a gate in the wall.

8. Turn left along the road to the priory and start.

Facilities:

Toll road to large parking area on the headland at Penmon Point (*Trwyn Du*). Seasonal cafe and toilets near the end of the toll road.

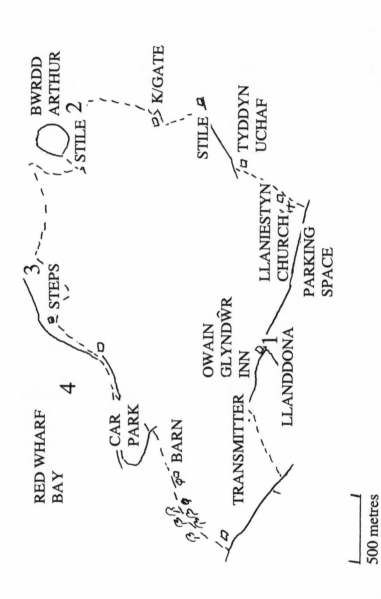

RED WHARF BAY

BWRDD ARTHUR

STILE 2

K/GATE

STILE

TYDDYN UCHAF

3

STEPS

4

CAR PARK

BARN

LLANIESTYN CHURCH

PARKING SPACE

OWAIN GLYNDŴR INN

1

TRANSMITTER

LLANDDONA

500 metres

Llanddona – Llaniestyn – Bwrdd Arthur – Red Wharf Bay (Traeth Coch) – Llanddona

OS Maps:	1:50 000 Landranger Sheet 114; 1:25 000 Pathfinder Sheet 735, 751.
Start:	Owain Glyndwr Inn, Llanddona, G.R. 576797.
Access:	Llanddona is on a minor road off the B5109, north-west of Beaumaris. Buses from Bangor and Menai Bridge.
Parking:	Parking space at road bend and lane fork on outskirts of village.
Grade:	Moderate – field, scrub and woodland paths, beach, tracks and lanes.
Time:	3½ hours.

Points of Interest:

1. Llanddona at one time was famous for its witches. During the 16th century a group of strangers, men and women, arrived in a boat without oars in Red Wharf Bay *(Traeth Coch)*. It was thought they had come from Scandinavia and had been cast adrift for practising witchcraft. The people of Llanddona tried to drive them away but relented when – according to the legend – the witches caused a spring of pure water to appear on the sands. They settled in the district and built cottages on the hill slope between Llanddona and the sea. The men survived by smuggling whilst the women obtained their needs by begging and cursing. It was said that the men were ferocious fighters and when they became tired they released a black fly from their cravats which attacked their opponents eyes and blinded them. Nobody ever refused the women anything for fear of being cursed; they could visit a farmhouse and ask for a loaf of broad or whatever they wanted with no risk of refusal. A witch called Sian Bwt was only 4 feet tall and she had two thumbs on her left hand. The most feared

was Bela Fawr. Everything that went wrong in the village, such as an animal sick or dying, was blamed on the witches.

2. The path to Bwrdd Arthur is not actually a right of way but at the present time there appears to be no objection to its use. A natural fortress, surrounded by steep slopes, the limestone plateau covers 17 acres. The English translation of Bwrdd Arthur is Arthur's Table. Another name for the fort is Din Silwy. It is defended by a wall of limestone slabs, 8 feet thick in places, which encircles the entire hilltop. Some hut circles can be seen close to the wall. Finds include 3rd and 4th century pottery and Roman coins. The fortress was probably built in pre-Roman times and was reoccupied at various times during the Roman period. From the plateau, in clear conditions, views are superb with the Lake District hills visible across the Irish Sea. Lime-loving plant can be found here – such as rock rose and wild basil.

3. This National Trust property called Bryn Offa is a small common on a limestone hill with wide views over Red Wharf Bay. It is known for its lime-loving wild flowers. In late spring and early summer look for burnet rose, saw-wort, dog rose and honeysuckle – and also the attendant butterflies.

4. The Welsh name for the bay, Traeth Coch, means Red Beach. It is said to date back to around 1170 when a frenzied battle with Viking warriors left the sands so saturated with blood, the bay took on a red hue. The name Red Wharf Bay comes from the 18th century when the western side of the bay was busy with a quay, shipyard and quarry. During the 2nd World War it was feared that the enemy might land in the bay and to prevent such an invasion large poles were placed in the sand. At low tide the bay looks inviting with ten square miles of exposed sand. However, it is dangerous to cross the sands, especially on an incoming tide when the channels and pools fill very rapidly.

Walk Directions: (-) denotes Point of Interest

1. In Llanddona (1) take the road opposite the village shop and Owain Glyndwr pub (not the lane signposted Traeth – although it leads to an alternative start and parking place). Continue to where the road bends

left at a signpost for Llaniestyn Church.

2. Turn right (parking space here). In a few paces fork right and follow the lane for about 800 metres to reach a track on the left which leads to the church.

3. Before the churchyard cross a stile on the right and descend the field to another stile on the right of farm buildings.

4. Cross the middle of the field to a kissing-gate and follow the right edge of the next field to a lane near Tyddyn Uchaf farm.

5. Turn right for about 500 metres. Before a farm on the left cross a stile and take the track ahead. Continue through fields and in front of a farmhouse turn right to a kissing-gate. Cross the next field to a gate and turn right on the track to a lane.

6. Turn left and follow the lane to a left bend. Bear right over a stile. Here a path on the right climbs to the fort of Bwrdd Arthur (2).

7. Return to the stile and continue on the path. Just before a farm turn left on a track and follow it into a field. Bear right keeping to the right edge of two fields. A path through the bushes leads to a stile and National Trust land (3).

8. Descend the slope to a track. Turn left and follow it to a track junction at a house. Bear right and right again at a fork. Just before a cottage ahead bear left up steps to a gate.

9. Bear slightly right to a stile and continue in the same direction to a corner kissing-gate above the cliffs.

10. Continue to a kissing-gate on the right of a cottage garden. The path leads to steps and the beach of Red Wharf Bay *(Traeth Coch)* (4). Turn left.

11. After following the beach a short distance go up to the track above it and continue in the same direction. Pass a car park and kiosk.

12. Continue on the lane as it bears left away from the beach. After a left bend on the hill pass a track on the left. At the next track on the right go through a kissing-gate.

13. Continue to where the track bends left. Leave it and keep ahead to

follow a wall on the left. Pass a barn and continue on a path through woodland.

14. After passing through open land the path re-enters woods. It follows a fairly level course and eventually reaches a track at some houses. Turn left to a lane.

15. Turn left. Pass a track to Bryn Castell on the right and shortly go up steps on the left to a footpath.

16. Follow the path through rocky outcrops and gorse to a kissing-gate. Climb to the right over some rocks then bear left towards a transmitter.

17. Pass the transmitter on the left and bear left to follow its fence to a kissing-gate and lane. Turn right.

18. Ignore a track on the left by a house. At a lane junction turn left and follow the lane to the road in Llanddona. Turn left to the start.

Facilities:

Car park at Red Wharf Bay *(Traeth Coch)*. Kiosk and toilets near the beach and car park. Pub and village shop in Llanddona.

Benllech – Cors Goch – Llanfair Mathafarn Eithaf – Pant y Saer – Benllech

OS Maps:	1:50 000 Landranger Sheet 114; 1:25 000 Pathfinder Sheet 735.
Start:	Benllech, A5025/B5108 crossroads, G.R. 518828.
Access:	Benllech is on the A5025, about 8 miles north of Menai Bridge (Porthaethwy). Buses from Bangor, Menai Bridge and Amlwch.
Parking:	Car park near the crossroads at the start.
Grade:	Moderate – paths, tracks and lanes.
Time:	3½ hours.

Points of Interest:

1. Benllech is a popular Anglesey resort which is well-known for its sandy beach and safe bathing. This large village expanded on the arrival of the railway to Red Wharf Bay, making it accessible as a holiday destination. The branch line opened in 1909 only to close to pedestrian traffic in 1930 and never reached Benllech as was intended. In previous centuries most of the activity around Benllech was centred on its quarries. Stone quarried in the area was used in the building of Beaumaris and Caernarfon Castles. Later exports were millstones and a high quality black and grey marble.

2. This is the Cors Goch Nature Reserve managed by the North Wales Wildlife Trust. The valley was formed by geological faulting and glacial erosion. There are areas of fenland, limestone grassland, heath, scrub and lake, providing different habitats for a diverse range of plants and animals. A number of orchids may be found and also the small, carnivorous plant, butterwort. Many species of butterflies are here including fritillaries, green-veined white, ringlet, peacock and

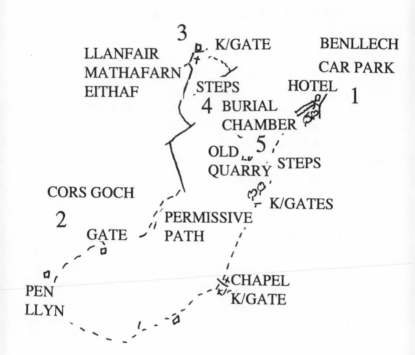

BENLLECH

3   K/GATE   CAR PARK

LLANFAIR   HOTEL
MATHAFARN   1
EITHAF   STEPS

        4 BURIAL
           CHAMBER

           OLD   5
CORS GOCH QUARRY STEPS

2   K/GATES

    GATE   PERMISSIVE
            PATH

PEN   CHAPEL
LLYN   K/GATE

                              ┕━━━━━━━┙
                              500 metres

common blue. Several kinds of dragonfly are found on the reserve and also day flying moths such as the emperor moth. Not so visible is the medicinal leech. Because of the density of the reedbeds, birds are probably more likely to be heard than seen. Birds on the reserve include heron, grebe, ruddy duck, curlew, snipe, coot, moorhen, warblers, reed bunting and barn owl. The reserve is also home to the water shrew.

3. George Borrow came here in 1854 on his tour of Wild Wales. He wanted to see the parish birthplace of Goronwy Owen, a famous Welsh poet. George Borrow climbed over the churchyard walls to find the church locked, but discovered kind hearts close by and was shown the house where Goronwy Owen had lived. Goronwy's life is a story of disappointment and tragedy. Born on New Year's Day in 1723, he attended schools in Wales before going to Jesus College Oxford in 1742. After being ordained he was curate at Llanfair Mathafarn Eithaf for a few weeks and was greatly disappointed when he had to leave because the Bishop had promised the position to someone else. Goronwy moved to Oswestry, became a curate, married and wrote much poetry, mainly religious. After a number of moves, the death of a daughter, financial problems and help from the Morris brothers (see Walk 7), he moved to London. From there, in 1757, he sailed to a job in Virginia, America. The conditions on board ship were so horrific that his wife and younger child died during the voyage. After arrival in America he eventually remarried. His new wife soon died and also his son, Goronwy. He married yet again, had more children, became the owner of a tobacco and cotton plantation but died himself in 1769. One of his greatest poems was in praise of Anglesey, Cywydd Hiraeth am Fôn *(Longing for Anglesey)*.

4. The remains of 54 persons, men, women and children, were found during excavation of this small Neolithic burial chamber. It is likely that the burials were made over a long period of time. Arrowheads and pieces of Neolithic pottery were also found and next to the chamber there was a large pot containing bones and pottery, suggestive of some kind of ritual or offering.

5. The narrow, overgrown path heads in the direction of the Pant y

Saer hut group. Partly overgrown, the site has an enclosure wall, two round huts and a couple of rectangular buildings adjoining the eastern hut. Excavation yielded pieces of pottery and querns and also a brooch of the 5th or 6th century AD.

Walk Directions: (-) denotes Point of Interest

1. Starting at the crossroads in Benllech (1) walk along the A5025 in the direction of Menai Bridge *(Porthaethwy)*. Just beyond the Glanrafon Hotel turn right on the road for Ty'n-y-gongl.

2. Almost immediately turn left on a footpath. Keep ahead through trees with a stream on the right. Go up steps and continue ahead through fields to a stile and lane.

3. Turn left and, in a few paces, look for steps on the right. Follow the left boundary of the field with, at first, an old quarry on the right.

4. When the quarry edge bears away to the right be sure to keep to the left boundary of the field. Keep ahead into another field and continue to a clearing in some gorse. Take a path left through bushes to a kissing-gate.

5. Turn right on a path and, in a few paces, go left through a kissing-gate. Follow a clear path through low scrub. Bear left through a field and go uphill into trees to reach a ladder stile. Continue to a kissing-gate on the right of a bungalow. Cross a field to a similar gate.

6. Turn right on the track to a chapel at a road. Cross directly to a kissing-gate. Follow the left edge of the field to an enclosed path. Bear right.

7. Follow this enclosed path until it emerges in a field. Cross to a kissing-gate. Turn right and at the field boundary go through a gap in the wall. Turn left to have a low wall on the left. Follow the path between bushes and walls to a stone stile.

8. Pass a house on the left and bear left to a stile. Follow another old enclosed way to a field. Keep ahead to a ladder stile. Continue by the left edge of the field to a kissing-gate and track.

9. Turn left to a track junction. Turn right on the track, which is

metalled in places. After passing a few houses it bends right and goes past the drive to Pen-llyn. Descend to have a marsh on the left (2).

10. When the track bends right to a house keep ahead through a gate and follow the permissive path through the Cors Goch Nature Reserve. In about 800 metres a short diversion may be taken along a board walk in the reed beds. Continue on the main path to a track then bear left and keep left to the road.

11. Turn left to another road. Turn right and take the first lane left.

12. At a lane junction bear right to Llanfair Mathafarn Eithaf Church (3). Continue past the churchyard and just before a house turn right down a drive.

13. At a gate ahead turn right through a kissing-gate. After crossing a stream follow the left edges of fields to an enclosed path. Join a track and follow it to a road.

14. Turn right and in a few metres go left up steps to a footpath. Emerge in a field and bear right to a stile. Slant left to the next stile near a corner and keep ahead through gorse to the Pant y Saer burial chamber (4).

15. Go left downhill to pick up a clear path which bears right and descends to a field. Follow the left edge to a kissing-gate and track.

16. Turn left and at a fork bear right uphill. Where the track bends left to a house keep ahead to a kissing-gate. In a few metres notice a path on the left (5).

17. Continue on the main path to a road. Turn right and at a junction bear right again to the main road. Turn left past the Glanrafon Hotel to the start in Benllech.

Facilities:

Another car park near the library. Full facilities in Benllech. Toilets in the car park at the start. Several campsites in the area.

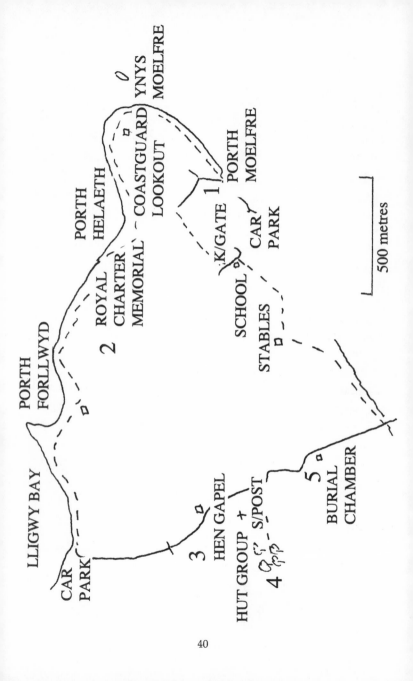

LLIGWY BAY

CAR PARK

PORTH FORLLWYD

PORTH HELAETH

0

YNYS MOELFRE

COASTGUARD LOOKOUT

PORTH MOELFRE

1

K/GATE

CAR PARK

ROYAL CHARTER MEMORIAL

2

SCHOOL

STABLES

HEN GAPEL

3

4 S/POST

HUT GROUP

5

BURIAL CHAMBER

500 metres

Moelfre – Traeth Lligwy
– Din Lligwy – Moelfre

OS Maps:	1:50 000 Landranger Sheet 114; 1:25 000 Pathfinder Sheet 735.
Start:	Moelfre harbour, G.R. 513863.
Access:	Moelfre is near the A5025, about 10 miles north of Menai Bridge (Porthaethwy).
Parking:	Car park behind the shops.
Grade:	Moderate – cliff and field paths, lane.
Time:	2½-3 hours.

Points of Interest:

1. Behind the kiosk but close to the road, is the anchor from the coaster Hindlea which was wrecked off Moelfre Point on 27 October 1959. Caught in a violent storm the empty cargo boat was sheltering in Dulas Bay when the wind changed suddenly from the south-west to north and the Hindlea started to drag anchor. The coxswain of Moelfre lifeboat answered the call for assistance although he did not have time to collect a full crew and had to use the unfamiliar reserve boat. The regular lifeboat was away being refitted. In a hurricane, through 25 foot waves, he skilfully manoeuvred the lifeboat up to the Hindlea's port quarter. The manoeuvre was repeated eight times and on each run a member of the Hindlea's crew leapt into the lifeboat. Shortly after the 500 ton cargo boat was smashed against the rocks and broken in two. For this dramatic rescue the lifeboat crew received RNLI medals.

2. The Royal Charter, a luxurious steamship, was one of the fastest clippers of her time. She had set sail from Melbourne, Australia, for Liverpool on 20 August 1859. Many of her passengers were gold diggers, returning with their fortunes. On the evening of 25 October, when the ship was rounding The Skerries, the wind veered to the

north-east and she had to battle against the hurricane force wind. The ship strived on and off Point Lynas rockets were sent up and a gun fired, although it would have been impossible for any boat to put out. Anchors were dropped but the chains parted and in the early hours of 26 October the ship struck a ledge under the cliffs of Moelfre. By dawn local people were on the cliffs and were able to assist the survivors. More than 450 people perished and no women or children were saved. For sometime afterwards gold was washed up on the pebble beaches and in the rock pools around Moelfre. The Hindlea was wrecked near the same spot 100 years later.

3. Enclosed by a low stone wall, this small roofless chapel dates from the 12th century. The base of the walls remain from that period whilst the nave and chancel were rebuilt in the 14th century. Inside the south chapel, which was added 200 years later, a flight of steps lead down to a small crypt.

4. The Din Lligwy hut group was probably the home of a local chieftain around the 4th century AD. The walls of the enclosure are five foot thick and the site covers about half an acre. There are two large round huts and a number of rectangular buildings, all of which would have been thatched. The round huts were the main living quarters and the finds in one of them included pottery, glassware and a silver ingot. The presence of smelting hearths and iron slag in some of the rectangular buildings indicate that they were used as workshops. The others were barns or possibly pens for animals. Excavations, lasting several years from 1905, uncovered Roman coins dated 270-350 AD, many pieces of pottery and teeth of domesticated animals.

5. At first glance, the Din Lligwy burial chamber looks as if it is resting on the ground. The huge capstone, measuring roughly 18 feet by 16 feet is supported by stones to raise it just above ground level. A large chamber lies beneath it and its entrance is on the eastern side. Excavation in 1909 discovered the unburnt bones of 15-30 men, women and children. They were in two groups, separated by a layer of stones. At the bottom there was a bed of mussel shells, whilst the upper layer of bones was covered with the shells of limpets. Animal bones and flints were found plus pieces of broken Beaker pottery,

which suggests that the chamber was erected close to the end of the Neolithic period. The whole tomb would have been covered by a mound of stones or earth.

Walk Directions: (-) denotes Point of Interest

1. Start at the harbour (1) and walk uphill with the sea on the right. When the road bends left, turn right on a lane above the sea.

2. Continue on a footpath. Pass Moelfre lifeboat station and cross a small beach. Go through a kissing-gate on to the headland. Offshore lies a small island, Ynys Moelfre.

3. Walk past the coastguard lookout and continue on the cliff path. On reaching a caravan site look for a marker post and bear right down steps to a kissing-gate. The path descends and passes behind the shingle beach of Porth Helaeth.

4. On the ascent from the beach look for steps on the left. These lead to a stone memorial commemorating the loss of the Royal Charter in 1859 (2).

5. Continue on the cliff path. At Porth Forllwyd the path turns inland, avoiding private land.

6. The path returns to the cliffs. Continue, with fine views over the long beach of Traeth Lligwy, to reach a car park at a refreshment hut.

7. Bear left past the hut and continue along a road. At crossroads keep ahead, uphill. Look for a signpost on the right to Din Lligwy and Hen Gapel.

8. To visit the monuments follow the left edge of the field. Hen Gapel (3) is on the right.

9. In the next field the path bears right to a kissing-gate. Take the path through the copse to Din Lligwy (4).

10. Return to the lane and turn right. In 300 metres a kissing-gate gives access to Lligwy burial chamber (5).

11. Continue on the lane. Just before the bottom of the hill and the stream, turn left over a low stone stile.

12. Walk along the right edge of two fields, with the stream on the right. Cross a stile and in the 3rd field slant left to the next stile. Continue, slanting left towards buildings. Cross a stile in the far corner of the field.

13. Turn right and follow a drive. It bends left to emerge at a school and road.

14. Turn left and shortly bear right through a kissing-gate. Cross the middle of the field to reach an enclosed path. Follow it to some steps beside a cottage.

15. Keep ahead and join a road. Continue ahead and follow the road as it bends right and left. Walk past the Post Office downhill to Moelfre harbour.

Facilities:

Alternative car park at Traeth Lligwy which has a seasonal kiosk and toilets. Plenty of refreshment places in Moelfre especially near the harbour. Toilets in the car park behind the shops. The Seawatch Centre is near the cliff path.

Traeth Lligwy – Traeth yr Ora – Mynydd Bodafon – Penrhosllugwy – Traeth Lligwy

OS Maps:	1:50 000 Landranger Sheet 114; 1:25 000 Pathfinder Sheet 735.
Start:	Car park at Traeth Lligwy, G.R. 492873.
Access:	Take the A5025 to Brynrefail, which is 5 miles south of Amlwch. Follow the signposted lane to Traeth Lligwy.
Parking:	Car park at Traeth Lligwy.
Grade:	Strenuous – coast, field, scrub and hill paths, lane.
Time:	3½ hours.

Points of Interest:

1. Straight ahead, about a mile offshore, lie the hazardous rocks of Ynys Dulas. The island is part of a reef, most of which is invisible. Built in 1824, the tower on the island includes a fireplace and at one time it was stocked with food for shipwrecked sailors. Several ships have come to grief on the reef including the schooner Clagan in 1917. The only survivors were the cabin boy and ship's dog.

2. The granite cross commemorates four remarkable brothers who lived in the 18th century. They were the sons of a local cooper who lived on a farm overlooking Dulas Bay. Lewis Morris (1701-1765) trained to be a surveyor and became a customs officer at Holyhead. He took on the difficult task of a hydrographic survey of the Welsh coast from the Orme to South Wales, which he completed in 1748. He was also a poet and scholar. Richard Morris (1703-1779) went to live in London and was a clerk in the navy. He founded the Honourable Society of Cymmrodorion which supported Welsh scholarship and culture. William Morris (1705-1763) did not leave Anglesey. He spent his life as a customs official in Holyhead and became a well-known botanist and gardener. John Morris (1706-1740) left Anglesey to join

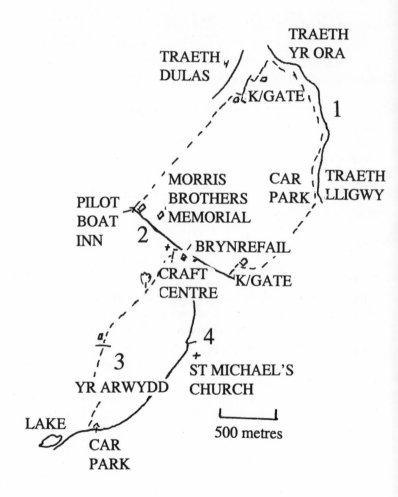

TRAETH
YR ORA

TRAETH
DULAS

K/GATE

1

MORRIS
BROTHERS
MEMORIAL

CAR
PARK

TRAETH
LLIGWY

PILOT
BOAT
INN

2

BRYNREFAIL

CRAFT
CENTRE

K/GATE

4

3

ST MICHAEL'S
CHURCH

YR ARWYDD

LAKE

500 metres

CAR
PARK

the navy. The brothers were enthusiastic letter writers and kept in touch with one another, and others, by correspondence. Many of their letters survive and these give an insight into the social life of 18th century Anglesey.

3. Although the highest summit on Mynydd Bodafon, Yr Arwydd, is only 178 metres, the abrupt, rocky nature of this rugged hill gives an impression of much greater height. Its rocks are composed of ancient Pre-Cambrian quartzite and most of the hill is covered with heather and gorse. Look and listen for heathland birds such as skylark, meadow pipit, wheatear, stonechat, yellowhammer and whitethroat. On clear days views extend to Snowdonia, the Lake District and the mountains of Ireland.

4. This little parish church has undergone much restoration but is well worth a visit. Dedicated to St Michael, it dates back to the 15th century. Inside, on the south side of the chancel, rests a 6th century stone with a Latin inscription. A medieval stoup is by the north door. Brown long-eared bats make use of the church.

Walk Directions: (-) denotes Point of Interest

1. From the car park take a footpath that starts in the dunes at the back of Lligwy beach. Continue, with the sea on your right, until the path goes down to the small beach called Porth y Môr (1).

2. Ignore a stile on the left. Walk along the beach and shortly take a path that goes up on the cliffs again. Follow it to the sandy beach of Traeth yr Ora.

3. Above the beach, behind a seat, a footpath leads to a farmhouse. Continue on a track and turn left at a lane.

4. Just before the lane bends left, turn right on an enclosed path to a kissing-gate. Follow the left edges of fields to a ladder stile and track.

5. Where the track bends right cross the ladder stile ahead. Follow the right edge of the field to a stile behind the Pilot Boat Inn.

6. Turn left on the road. In about 250 metres look for a kissing-gate on the left. It leads to the Morris Brothers Memorial (2).

7. Continue on the road to Brynrefail. Take a railed path on the right beside the Welsh Craft Centre. Walk along a lane and at the end of the first field on the right go up steps to a small gate.

8. Follow the left edge of two fields and go up steps into trees. Keep left to a ladder stile.

9. Head towards a house with two chimneys. Keep uphill to pass a fence on the left and reach a ladder stile. Follow the left edge of the next field to a stile in the wall.

10. Keep left by an old fence. Continue ahead over stiles and a footbridge in the direction of Mynydd Bodafon.

11. Continue towards a group of houses. Cross a stile into a field and follow the right edge to a stile at a garden.

12. Go through the garden to a gate. Keep ahead to another track. Cross directly over to a path that climbs through heather and gorse.

13. When the path starts to descend, turn left on a path to the summit of Yr Arwydd (3).

14. From the summit take a path south in the direction of a lake. Descend to a small parking area and turn left to the lane. To visit the lakeside, turn right.

15. Retrace your steps from the lake and walk downhill on the lane. Continue to a sharp left bend. The church of Penrhosllugwy (4) is on the right.

16. Continue on the lane to the A5025. Turn right and after about 400 metres go through a kissing-gate on the left. Keep ahead through fields and continue on a path that bends right at a fence near a house.

17. Cross a track to a ladder stile and field. Go through the gate ahead and follow a clear path through gorse to eventually reach a track. Turn left to the car park at the start.

Facilities:

Small car park near Mynydd Bodafon. Pub on route (Pilot Boat Inn). Seasonal kiosk and toilets at Traeth Lligwy.

Amlwch Port (Porth Amlwch) – Llaneilian – Point Lynas – Mynydd Eilian – Amlwch Port (Porth Amlwch)

OS Maps:	1:50 000 Landranger Sheet 114; 1:25 000 Pathfinder Sheet 733.
Start:	Car park above Amlwch harbour, G.R. 453936.
Access:	From the A5025 follow the road signs to Amlwch Port. Buses from Bangor, Holyhead and Llangefni.
Parking:	Amlwch Port.
Grade:	Strenuous – cliff and field paths, lanes.
Time:	4 hours.

Points of Interest:

1. The narrow, natural harbour was enlarged about 200 years ago to accommodate the vessels which exported copper from the mines on Parys Mountain. Some of the excavated rock was used to build the pier and face the dock wall. The walls are built of vertically placed stone which is unusual in Anglesey and the method may have been introduced to Amlwch by Cornishmen seeking work in the copper mines.

2. The remains of a square, walled enclosure is just visible under a large rock, a short distance from the stream. This is the site of Ffynnon Eilian, the well of St Eilian. For many centuries it was believed that the well water could cure various ailments. Drinking the water was followed by rituals of prayer at the well and offerings placed in the church. More recently, the well has been used as a cursing well. One practice was to scratch the cursed person's initials on a piece of slate and place it in the well.

3. Eilian is said to have landed at Porth yr Ychen in the 6th century.

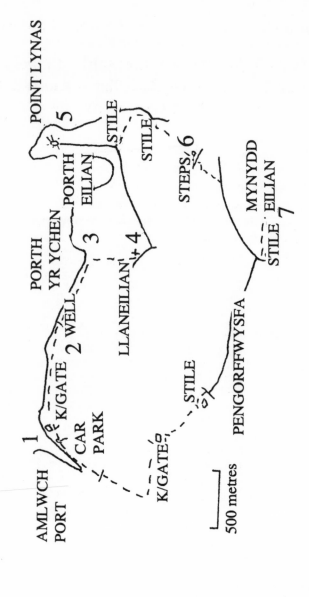

He came from Rome with his family and cattle and built a church nearby. Eilian had to excommunicate and blind Caswallon Law Hir *(Caswallon the Long Handed)* who had commited a misdemeanour. However, Caswallon was forgiven, his sight restored, and in return, Eilian was given land to build his church. He could have all the land crossed by his hart before it was caught by Caswallon's hounds. Starting at Dulas, the chase went to Parys Mountain and finished at Llam y Carw *(Hart's Leap)* where the deer escaped the dogs by jumping across the gorge. The land St Eilian was given for his church comprised this corner of Anglesey bounded by Dulas, Parys Mountain and Amlwch to Point Lynas.

4. The oldest part of St Eilian's Church is the 12th century tower which has a pyramid shaped roof. Most of the remainder of the church was rebuilt in the 15th century. A short 17th century passage joins the chancel to the small chapel of St Eilian. On the rood-screen there is a lugubrious painting of a skeleton.

5. In the 18th century the Mersey pilots had a watch-house here with a light consisting of a candle with two reflectors. It was replaced in 1835 by the present lighthouse which now has an automatic beacon. This is a good site to watch birds on migration – in late summer gannets, skuas and manx shearwaters fly past the headland. Sometimes there is a glimpse of a dolphin or porpoise.

6. The white building above here was once a semaphore station, one of a chain between Holyhead and Liverpool. During the 18th and 19th centuries ship owners and merchants were in need of some kind of news system to let them know their ships and cargo were approaching Liverpool. The first signal was on Bidston Hill for ships entering the River Mersey. The system was extended and in 1827 communication by semaphore was established between Liverpool and Holyhead. The apparatus consisted of a visual code on moveable arms.

7. From Mynydd Eilian there are fine views of northern Anglesey, Holyhead Mountain and the mainland. On very clear days it may be possible to see the mountains of the Lake District and southern Ireland. Much closer is the scarred hill of Parys Mountain, where copper extraction began in the Bronze Age. Recent excavation has

uncovered primitive stone hammers dating 2000-1500 BC. Ingots of copper with Roman inscriptions have been found on the side of the mountain. The greatest activity came in the 18th century when two mines, the Parys Mine and the Mona Mine, were operating on the mountain and exporting all over the world. Copper was used to make nails and bolts and to sheathe the hulls of wooden ships to reduce damage by marine organisms. Amlwch's harbour was enlarged and the town's population swelled to 6000. The conspicious windmill on the mountain's summit was built in 1878 to assist in pumping water, a source of copper. Water was pumped from the workings into ponds containing scrap iron. Chemical reaction between the copper solution and iron caused the copper to precipitate out resulting in a sludge of copper, which was dried and smelted. The water, without its copper but rich in iron, was channelled into pools and it deposited yellow ochre, used in paint. These precipitation pits and ochre pools can be seen on the east and south sides of Parys Mountain.

Walk Directions: (-) denotes Point of Interest

1. From the car park above Amlwch harbour (1) walk towards a house and go through a kissing-gate on the right.

2. Follow the narrow path along the coast to a ladder stile and cross a stream (2). Continue on the coast path and after passing through a small gate cross a stile at Porth yr Ychen (3).

3. Don't cross the stile ahead. Bear right to follow the right edge of the field uphill to a track. Go through a gate and farmyard. Take the left-hand of two gates. Cross steps to reach the lane and Llaneilian Church (4).

4. Turn left at the church and left again. Walk downhill to the slipway at Porth Eilian.

5. Bear right and follow the road the Point Lynas lighthouse (5).

6. Return along the road to some gateposts. In about another 100 metres turn left to a stile.

7. Follow the wall on the right and at a corner keep ahead to the coast.

Bear right, with the sea on the left, and at the next fence ignore the stile nearest the sea but go uphill to the ladder stile.

8. Continue uphill to a kissing-gate. Bear right and follow the right boundary to the next kissing-gate. Go half-left to a marker post below a gorse bush and continue to a ladder stile.

9. The path bears right through gorse. Reach a marker post and continue to a wall (6). Bear right to an enclosed track. Pass a barn and reach a stile.

10. Cross a track and go up steps. Take a path to the corner of a high wall. Continue with the wall on the left to a kissing-gate. Bear right to cross a field and keep ahead to a building and walled path. Join a track and follow it uphill to a lane.

11. Turn right on the lane. Where the lane bends right go left on a narrow road. In a few paces bear left to a stile. Follow the path to the trig point on Mynydd Eilian (7).

12. Return to the narrow road and lane. Turn left downhill to Pengorffwysfa. Bear right and immediately left in the direction of Amlwch.

13. At the next road junction turn right and in a few paces go left on a track. Pass to the right of a house to reach a ladder stile.

14. Follow an enclosed path to a field. Bear right between rock outcrops and aim for the roof of a house seen in trees ahead. Go through a wall gap and follow a wall on the left. Reach another wall and bear left to follow the wall on the right to a stile.

15. Turn right to reach a track coming from the house. Keep ahead and when the track bends right, turn left to a kissing-gate.

16. Follow the left fence. At the field corner ignore a kissing-gate on the left but go through the one ahead.

17. After passing through gorse bear left to follow a wall on the left. Cross a broken low gate and stream to reach a path junction.

18. Turn right on a clear path. Ignore a path on the right and turn left to a kissing-gate at houses.

19. Keep ahead to a road. Turn left then right to pass the Adelphi.

20. Fork left to the slipway. Take a path on the right and continue along the harbour. Bear right up steps and walk past the old Shell buildings to the car park.

Facilities:

Full facilities in Amlwch. Toilets near Porth Eilian. Camping at Llaneilian.

Bull Bay (Porthllechog) – Mynydd Pantygaseg – Porth Wen – Bull Bay (Porthllechog)

OS Maps:	1:50 000 Landranger Sheet 114; 1:25 000 Pathfinder Sheet 733.
Start:	Bull Bay harbour, G.R. 426944.
Access:	Bull Bay (Porthllechog) is off the A5025 about 2 miles west of Amlwch.
Parking:	Small car park on minor road near the harbour at Bull Bay. Buses from Amlwch and Holyhead.
Grade:	Easy – field and cliff paths.
Time:	1½-2 hours.

Points of Interest:

1. Bull Bay *(Porthllechog)* was once a busy, little fishing port and ships were built here in the 19th century. It also had a pilot station with two four-oared boats. Steamers from Liverpool used to call at the northern end of the bay to land passengers and stores.

2. The abandoned Porthwen brickworks is situated in a spectacular position on the west side of the bay. It closed about the time of the 1st World War. Quartzite from a quarry on Craig Wen, the hill behind, was send down an incline to the brickworks where it was made into silica bricks, which were used in the steel industry. They were exported by boat from the quay. The tall chimneys and beehive shaped kilns survive alongside the shell of the brickworks.

3. The small island called East Mouse *(Ynys Amlwch)* is visible ahead on the eastern side of Bull Bay. Between the island and the chemical works lies the wreck of the Dakota, a huge steamship which had been making the transatlantic crossing from Liverpool to New York in May 1877. The ship, built for speed, was steaming at 14 knots about two miles offshore when the course was changed. The ship should have

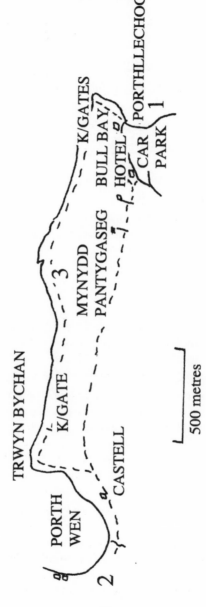

gone further from land but for some unfathomable reason she headed towards the coast and hit rocks. Bull Bay lifeboat rescued the passengers. Another wreck, close to Bull Bay but near the western side, is HMS Pansy. This Wallasey paddle steamer, taken over by the Admirality, sank in a north-easterly gale in 1916.

Walk Directions: (-) denotes Point of Interest

1. Leave the harbour (1) by taking the lane opposite. Pass the car park and picnic tables. Continue uphill past houses and, at a footpath signpost, take the private road on the right.

2. Where the road bends right, go left downhill on a narrow path through bushes. It rises to a stile.

3. Take the left path to a gate. To the right of it cross a stile. Bear right on the track and go left through a kissing-gate.

4. Cross the field to a stile and keep ahead to a track. Continue opposite on a path into a field. Keep to the right edge and go through a wide gap in the wall.

5. Continue to another wall gap and follow the crest of the ridge, Mynydd Pantygaseg. With the bay, Porth Wen, ahead descend to a kissing-gate at a corner.

6. Follow a wall on the left and at the corner bear left to reach a wide, green walled track.

7. The walk turns right here but for the best views (and photographs) of Porthwen brickworks (2) it is worthwhile to make this diversion. Go along the track, keep ahead, pass a house *(Castell)* on the right and follow a path up to the cliffs. Continue over a ladder stile and stream to some outcrops and a fine view of the brickworks. Return the same way.

8. Reach the cliffs and, with the sea on the left, continue around the headland, Trwynbychan, to reach a kissing-gate.

9. Continue on the coast path (3) and at a pair of kissing-gates go through the left gate.

10. Follow the path on to a little headland. Cross a stile to the right of

a house. Follow a track and shortly bear left on a footpath which descends to the harbour and starting place.

Facilities:

Toilets and picnic tables near the car park. The Bull Bay Hotel, near the start/end of the walk, is open to non-residents.

Cemaes Bay – Llanbadrig – Porth Llanlleiana – Dinas Gynfor – Porth Wen – Cemaes Bay

OS Maps:	1:50 000 Landranger Sheet 114; 1:25 000 Pathfinder Sheet 733.
Start:	Above the main beach, near the harbour, G.R. 373935.
Access:	Cemaes Bay is easily reached from the A5025, 5 miles west of Amlwch.
Parking:	Car park near the beach at Cemaes Bay.
Grade:	Strenuous – cliff and field paths, lane. Warning – the cliff path between Llanbadrig Church and Porth Llanlleiana is narrow and exposed. This section can be avoided by taking the alternative, inland route.
Time:	3½-4 hours.

Points of Interest:

1. Cemaes Bay is popular with families because of its safe, sandy beach and rock pools. Formerly spelt 'Cemais', the name changed to Cemaes Bay in 1911 to differentiate it from the Powys village called Cemais. It is the most northerly village in Wales and was the chief port in northern Anglesey previous to the expansion of Amlwch. Smuggling was common along the coast. The village was known for its salted herrings and in the 19th century shipbuilding became an industry when small schooners were built in the bay. A pier was completed in 1835, replacing the fishermen's small structure, and to this coal was imported. Exports included limestone and marble from Porth Padrig. In 1900 the pier was again rebuilt and extended although trade was declining because of the railway, new roads and reduced mining activity at Amlwch.

2. The cliffs on this side of the bay consist of sedimentary rocks with

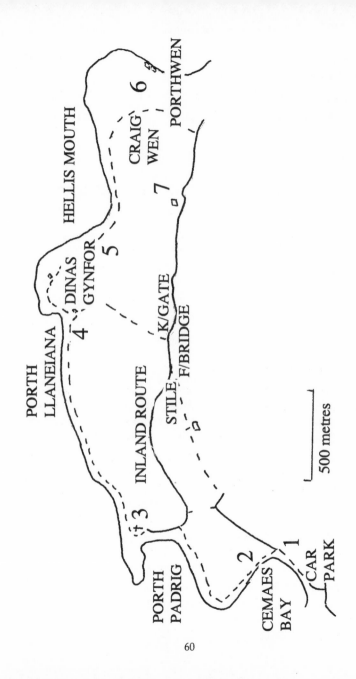

PORTH LLANEIANA

HELLIS MOUTH

PORTH PADRIG

DINAS GYNFOR

CRAIG WEN

PORTHWEN

INLAND ROUTE

STILE
F/BRIDGE
K/GATE

CEMAES BAY

CAR PARK

500 metres

1 2 3 4 5 6 7

60

alternate layers of limestone and sandstone. On the far side of the headland limestone was quarried and burnt in the limekiln for use as fertilizer. Gulls, fulmars and oystercatchers are commonly seen from the cliff path while spring and summer flowers are prolific. These include the blue sheep's bit, yellow cat's ear and purple knapweed.

3. Llanbadrig means church of St Patrick. According to local legend Patrick, a missionary, was shipwrecked on Ynys Badrig *(Middle Mouse)* and from there crossed to Anglesey. He found shelter in a cave, which is now below the churchyard, and in AD440 founded the church. The early church would have been built of timber; the present church dates from the 14th century. It was fully restored in the 19th century when the 3rd Lord Stanley of Alderley provided money for this. However, because Islam was his own faith, he insisted the church should contain Moslem elements. This influence is apparent in the predominance of the colour blue in the windows, the blue tiles and the Pastor Bonus mosaic. The church contains an ancient stone, the Icthus Stone, which was found under plaster during restoration work in 1884. It was probably a standing stone and sometime in the 7th-11th centuries acquired its Christian symbols. In 1985 the church was again restored after being set alight by vandals.

4. It is thought that a female recluse founded a chapel at Porth Llanlleiana about the 6th or 7th century. Many years ago excavation revealed female bones. The deserted ruins seen here today are from the 19th century china clay industry. The clay was dug from the hillside and shipped from the little harbour for use in the manufacture of porcelain.

5. The watchtower on Dinas Gynfor commemorates the coronation of Edward VII and it is situated on the most northerly headland in Wales. To the north-west is the island called Middle Mouse *(Ynys Badrig)*. The rocky promontory, surrounded by steep cliffs or slopes, made an ideal site for a hillfort in the Iron Age. The defence walls of Dinas Gynfor can be seen on the inland side. In the 19th century pebbles were found in a ditch on the site. These could have been ammunition for use in slings.

6. Porthwen brickworks closed at the beginning of the 1st World War. The hill behind, Craig Wen, provided quartzite for the manufacture of silica bricks, yellow bricks able to withstand very high temperatures. Although it had provided employment for local people, who walked daily from as far away as Amlwch, the works were never very successful. The biggest problems were the import of coal for the kilns and the transport of the bricks. A quay was built beside the works but the tides created difficulties and the bay is subject to swells, which caused the ships to strike rock on the seabed. Ship owners were refused insurance and this forced the closure of the works because no other form of transport was practicable.

7. Opposite a chapel, there is a house on the hillside called Bryn Llywelyn *(Llywelyn's Hill)*. This is thought to be the site of an ancient beacon used to summon Llywelyn's army. Further along the lane the wind turbines of Rhyd-y-groes can be seen in the distance. Wind power was a main source of energy in recent centuries and the stumps of old windmills are to be seen all over Anglesey. Some have been converted into houses.

Walk Directions: (-) denotes Point of Interest

1. From the car park (1) walk along the sea front to the east end of the bay. Turn left on the cliff path (2) and follow it through a number of kissing-gates to a lane at Porth Madrig.

2. Turn left to Llanbadrig Church (3).

3a. Cliff route. Take a path on the left which follows the churchyard wall on to the cliffs. Continue to the next headland and cross the wire fence. From here the path is narrow and exposed along steep slopes. Eventually, it bears right and drops down to a stile at Porth Llanlleiana (4).

3b. Inland route. Return along the lane and fork left at a junction. Continue over ½ mile and where the lane bends right turn left through a kissing-gate. Follow the left edge of fields downhill and cross a causeway through a marsh. Turn left to Porth Llanlleiana (4).

4. A path on the seaward side of the ruins climbs steeply to the top of the cliffs.

5. Continue along the promontory to the tower on the headland of Dinas Gynfor (5). After a fairly level section the path descends steeply to the next inlet, Hell's Mouth *(Porth Cynfor)*.

6. Cross a stile and climb a clear path, narrow in places. Beyond some winding gear bear right above the brickworks (6) and the bay called Porth Wen. Continue to an enclosed path leading to a lane.

7. Turn right on the lane (7). In about 1 mile turn left over a stone stile and descend to a footbridge. Keep ahead through fields to a stile on the right of buildings.

8. Cross a track to another stile. Bear left to a kissing-gate. Follow a fence on the right and continue on a clear path through a valley to a stone stile.

9. An enclosed path continues to a lane. Turn right and in a few paces take the lane left to Cemaes Bay and the start.

Facilities:

Alternative car park in the village. Another small car park is at the end of the bay. Toilets and kiosk by the main car park. Full facilities in the village. Cemaes Heritage Centre in the High Street. Camp site at Park Lodge.

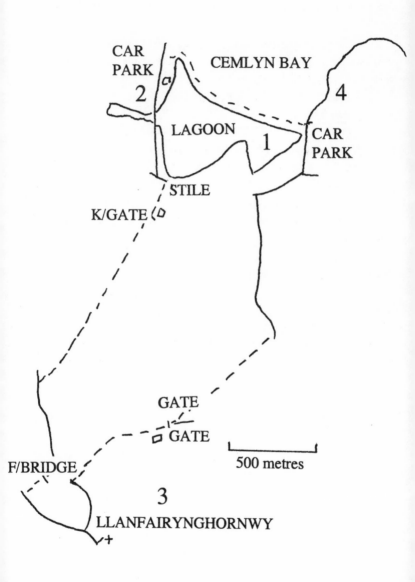

Cemlyn Bay – Bryn Aber
– Llanfairynghornwy – Cemlyn Bay

OS Maps:	1:50 000 Landranger Sheet 114; 1:25 000 Pathfinder Sheet 733.
Start:	Cemlyn Bay, eastern side, G.R. 336932.
Access:	Leave the A5025 1 mile west of Cemaes roundabout at Tregele, opposite the Douglas Inn. In 1½ miles turn right on a narrow lane which leads to a car park on the eastern side of Cemlyn Bay. Holyhead-Amlwch buses stop at Tregele, 1¾ miles from the start.
Parking:	Car park on the eastern side of Cemlyn Bay.
Grade:	Moderate – shingle beach, field paths, tracks and lane.
Time:	2½ hours.

Points of Interest:

1. Centuries of storms depositing pebbles high up on the Cemlyn Bay beach created the shingle ridge. A weir built in the 1930s, at the western end of the beach, turned an area of mud flats, pools and marsh into a lagoon. Because it is fed by freshwater streams and the incoming tide, the water of the lagoon is brackish and its level is maintained by the weir, which was reconstructed in 1978. The reserve was in private ownership until bought by the National Trust in 1971 and it is leased to the North Wales Wildlife Trust. A large colony of sandwich terns breed in the lagoon, along with common, artic and roseate terns. Red-breasted merganser, shelduck, mallard, coot, moorhen, oystercatcher, redshank and a number of small birds such as reed bunting and sedge warbler may be seen on the reserve. Large numbers of wildfowl, including goldeneye and little grebe, winter here. On the shingle ridge look for the white flowers of sea campion, the pink of thrift, the yellow horned poppy and sea kale.

2. The house behind the high wall is Bryn Aber, the former home of Captain Vivian Hewitt who created the reserve. A millionaire, he inherited his wealth from breweries. After a period of egg collecting from Welsh islands, including Puffin Island, Hewitt wished to settle in Anglesey and came to live at Bryn Aber, which was his home for 30 years until his death in 1965. Although an egg collector in his early years, he was passionate about birds and built the weir to form the lagoon. The purpose of the high walls at the house was to protect the trees and garden from salt laden winds and thus provide a garden bird sanctuary. His wish for herons to nest in the trees of the garden was granted before he died but, sadly, he was too ill at the time to see them. A man of diverse interests, he also collected traction engines, guns, stamps, coins and butterflies from all over the world. He was a pioneer aviator and made the first flight from the U.K. to Ireland in 1912. During the 2nd World War an untrue story spread that Hewitt was supplying German U-boats with fuel from tanks in his grounds and a detective from Scotland Yard came to investigate. The suspicious tanks were water tanks; Bryn Aber had no modern conveniences at that time. Captain Hewitt's land at Cemlyn was later bought by the National Trust from funds raised by Enterprise Neptune.

3. In the parish church at Llanfairynghornwy there is a memorial to Evan Thomas, the first of a long line of bone-setters. He lived on Anglesey from 1745 and died in 1814, but his origins are a mystery. It is said that one night, a local smuggler found a sinking vessel near Carmel Head *(Trwyn y Gader)* and close by there was a boat with two boys clinging to it. After rescue one boy died but the other went to live with Dr Lloyd at Mynachdy. Because he was a twin he was named Thomas, with the first name Evan. There is controversy about his nationality, he spoke a strange language, but it seems likely that he came from a Celtic area of Spain, such as Castile. As a child he treated a chicken's broken leg and Dr Lloyd allowed him to practise on his patients. He moved to Maes at Llanfairynghornwy and his reputation as a bone-setter spread. One of his patients was Lady Bulkeley of Baron Hill, Beaumaris, who suffered from arthritis. Evan's son, Richard Evans, became an accomplished bone-setter and all Richard's sons practised. The eldest son, Evan Thomas, set up as a bone-setter in

Liverpool at 3 Crosshall Street, treating dockworkers and seamen. Evans wanted his sons to be medically qualified and they attended the medical school at Edinburgh University. The eldest son, Hugh, was shocked by the amount of amputations performed on inflamed and diseased joints. He worked for a while with his father and then set up on his own at 11 Nelson Street, where he devised new methods of treatment including a special splint known as the Thomas Splint. Hugh Owen Thomas passed on his skills to a nephew, Robert Jones, who made his uncle's methods better known. Unfortunately, the teaching of Hugh Owen Thomas, who died in 1891, was not recognised whilst he was alive. Today he is remembered as an eminent orthopaedic surgeon. Robert Jones became Sir Robert Jones and worked with Dame Agnes Hunt to establish an orthopaedic hospital.

4. Near the car park a stile gives access to the rocky coast on the east side of Cemlyn Bay. An attractive route can be followed through heather, gorse and rock to Porth-y-Pistyll where Wylfa Nuclear Power Station looms close across the bay. The station, which has operated since 1971, has its own woodland nature trail, much frequented by owls.

Walk Directions: (-) denotes Point of Interest

1. Starting from the car park, either take the path alongside the lagoon (1) or, if it is the breeding season (April-July inclusive), follow the shingle beach to the far end.

2. Cross the stones over the inlet of the lagoon (during high tides this may be impossible) and bear left to follow a wall to a lane and car park.

3. Turn left past the house, Bryn Aber (2) , to a lane junction.

4. Turn left along the lagoon and look for a drive on the right. Cross the stone stile next to a gate and follow the drive. Continue past a house to a kissing-gate.

5. Follow the right edges of fields to a lane.

6. Turn left on the lane and in about ½ mile, before houses on the left, cross a stone stile on the right. Follow an enclosed path downhill to a

small bridge over a stream.

7. Go up to a kissing-gate and follow the right side of the field to a lane.

8. Turn left past houses and at a lane junction bear right to visit the church of Llanfairynghornwy (3). It is about 100 metres on the left.

9. Return from the church to the lane junction. Turn right and follow the lane signposted Cemlyn. In 400 metres look for a track on the right.

10. Follow this track– which has a cattle grid – to a house.

11. Keep ahead past the house to a little gate. Go down steps to a footbridge and cross into the field on the left.

12. Slant left across the field to a gate and cross the middle of the next field to a stile.

13. Follow the right edge of the field to a stile and continue through small fields to a lane.

14. Turn left on the lane and at a junction turn right. In about 250 metres turn left on the lane to the car park at the start (4).

Facilities:

Alternative car park on the western side of Cemlyn Bay. Wylfa Power Station has a visitor centre, picnic tables, guided tours and a nature trail.

Cemlyn Bay – Hen Borth – Carmel Head (Trwyn y Gader) – Penbrynyreglwys – Mynachdy – Cemlyn Bay

OS Maps:	1:50 000 Landranger Sheet 114; 1:25 000 Pathfinder Sheet 733.
Start:	Cemlyn Bay, western side, G.R. 329935.
Access:	Leave the A5025 1 mile west of Cemaes roundabout at Tregele, opposite the Douglas Inn. In 2 miles turn right, passing the Cemlyn lagoon on the right. Holyhead-Amlwch buses stop at Tregele, 2½ miles from the start.
Parking:	Car park on the western side of Cemlyn Bay.
Grade:	Strenuous – cliff and field paths, track and lane.
Time:	4½-5 hours.

Points of Interest:

1. The memorial commemorates the 150th anniversary of the first lifeboat on Anglesey. The founders, Reverend James Williams and his wife Frances, had witnessed the wreck of the vessel Alert on West Mouse, when 140 lives were lost. Frances Williams was so distressed by this tragedy that she established a fund to reward those who exerted themselves to save life. The first funds were raised by the selling of lithographic copies of one of her paintings. At the same time, about 1823, William Hillary of the Isle of Man wrote a pamphlet appealing for a National Institution for the Preservation of Life and Property from Shipwreck. This was to be the beginning of the RNLI. When Frances Williams and her husband heard of the institution they pleaded for one of the lifeboats to be sent to Anglesey. It was delivered to Cemlyn in 1828 and was stationed opposite Harry Furlough's Rocks. The same year saw the formation of the Anglesey Association for the Preservation of Life from Shipwreck. Some time

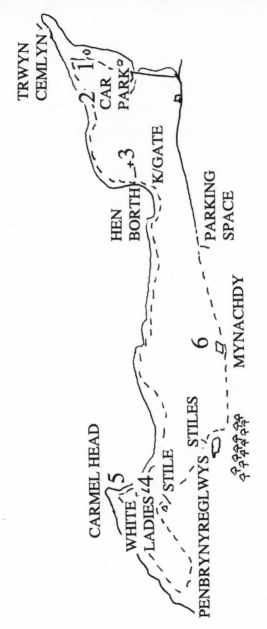

TRWYN CEMLYN

CAR PARK

HEN BORTH

K/GATE

PARKING SPACE

MYNACHDY

CARMEL HEAD

WHITE LADIES

STILE

STILES

PENBRYNYREGLWYS

500 metres

1
2
3
4
5
6

70

later, the Reverend James Williams saved 5 lives from the wrecked vessel Active in Cemaes Bay. He was awarded the gold medal of the RNLI, the first to be awarded in Wales. He carried out the rescue from the shore by taking a horse into the surf and throwing a grappling hook to the boat.

2. Look back for a view of Harry Furlough's Rocks off Trwyn Cemlyn. The Cemlyn lifeboat went to the assistance of the steamship Olinda when she hit a reef close to these rocks in 1854. She was on her way to South America when the Liverpool pilot, who was in charge, made the error of keeping close to the Anglesey coast instead of going seaward. Normally he disembarked at Lynas Point, but was prevented from doing so by the winter squall. His error lost the Olinda which still lies under the waves. Everybody was rescued.

3. The small, simple church, dedicated to St Rhwydrus, sits in the middle of fields close to a farm, Tyn Llan. The nave and font are Norman and the chancel was added in the 13th century. In the churchyard there are some interesting old gravestones; one is in the memory of a Norwegian Captain whose vessel was wrecked at Cemlyn in 1869.

4. This is one of two beacons known as the White Ladies. They act as a navigational aid when lined up with a similar beacon on the little island called West Mouse. The Welsh name for the island, lying one mile off shore, is Maen-y-Bugail – stone of the shepherd. This must be one of the most hazardous coastlines in Britain with its dangerous currents, underwater rocks and small islands. The barque Gilbert Thompson hit a reef close to West Mouse in 1881 when she was being pulled by a tug on her way home from Calcutta. All escaped except for the cabin boy who, because he had a broken leg, could not move quickly enough to leave the sinking ship. Only three people reached the shore alive when the Alert floundered on West Mouse in 1823.

5. Two miles off Carmel Head *(Trwyn y Gader)* are the cluster of islands known as The Skerries – a Viking name. The Welsh name is Ynysoedd y Moelrhoniaid, Seal Islands. These rocky islands, which are in the middle of a busy shipping route, have witnessed many shipwrecks. In 1675, Britain's first Royal Yacht, the Mary, was

wrecked here.

Presented to Charles II by the Mayor of Amsterdam, the Mary was a splendid vessel, very fast and luxuriously fitted out by Dutch craftsmen. She was transferred to the Royal Navy in 1661. On the foggy night on which she met doom, she was on passage from Dublin to Chester when she hit a rock on The Skerries. The Captain, the Earl of Meath and many passengers lost their lives. However, some sailors and passengers managed to reach an island, where they lit a fire with gun powder and timber from the wreck. After two days they were rescued by a passing vessel. When wrecked the Mary was carrying several bronze guns and these were discovered in 1971. Divers have also found other artefacts such as silver, coins, rings and lockets. The wreck site is now a protected one and diving is not normally allowed. In 1716 the first light, a coal beacon, was built on The Skerries by William Trench. All vessels, other than warships, that passed the islands were to pay him a penny per ton. The venture was a complete disaster. Trench's son drowned whilst taking coal out to The Skerries and the money paid did not even cover the cost of maintaining the beacon. After William Trench died an Act of Parliament was passed to enforce the dues – 1 penny per ton from British vessels and 2 from foreign ones. Distant relatives of Trench inherited the beacon and ealry in the 19th century the owner built a new lighthouse with an oil lantern. By 1835 it was extremely profitable. When Trinity House bought the lighthouse in 1841 the price paid was £444,984 11s 2d.

6. The National Trust own a large part of the Mynachdy Estate. Mynachdy means house of monks. The Cistercian Abbey of Aberconwy owned land here in the Middle Ages and monks may well have lived in a house here. According to a local legend, the cellars of the house had tunnels to caves in the cliffs where the monks hid their treasure. At one time the Mynachdy Estate included The Skerries. William Robinson of Mynachdy went for a boat trip to The Skerries with 12 companions in 1739 and on the return journey all were lost. The boat was found a few days later, empty, broken and oars missing, in a creek near Whitehaven, Cumbria. In a field near Mynachdy a biplane landed in 1910. The aviator was Robert Loraine who was making a trial flight from Blackpool to Holyhead in preparation for the

crossing of the Irish Sea. He was following the Anglesey coast but heat haze caused him to lose his way and 1 mile from land, near Carmel Head, his engine stopped. He glided to land safely in a field. In the following days wind prevented the machine becoming airborne. When at last he attempted to take off, the biplane crashed into a hummock causing so much damage it had to be rebuilt. A hangar was erected and hundreds of sightseers came to view the aircraft. Loraine's mechanics took almost a month to carry out repairs and then the next attempt at flight failed due to boggy ground. This time the machine was taken to Holyhead for repairs and a week later Loraine was on his way to Ireland. He failed to reach land – the biplane came down 200 yards from the Irish coast. In 1912 Vivian Hewitt made his successful crossing of the Irish Sea.

Walk Directions: (-) denotes Point of Interest

1. From the car park turn left along the track. Go past a memorial (1) on the right.

2. Reach the open land of Trwyn Cemlyn. Bear left with the wall to cross a stile. Turn right uphill (2).

3. Go through a gate with enormous stone posts and continue to a gate on the cliffs.

4. Bear left up the cliff and then descend over a series of stiles. The church dedicated to St Rhwydrus is across a field. To visit the church continue beside the cliffs to the end of the field and follow the arrow along the wall to stiles which give access to the churchyard (3).

5. Return to the cliff path and continue to the shingle beach of Hen Borth. Go through a kissing-gate and bear right over a stream. Ignore a kissing-gate on the left.

6. Go uphill and continue above cliffs and shingle beaches. In about two miles pass a white tower on the left (4).

7. Notice a tall chimney higher up on the left. This is past on the return. Continue around the coast to Carmel Head (*Trwyn y Gader*) (5).

8. Turn south to the headland of Trwyn Cerrigyreryr. From here there are fine views across Holyhead Bay.

9. Leave the coast and keep uphill over the highest point, Penbrynyreglwys. This was the site of a Roman beacon used as a warning for their fort and naval base at Caer Gybi *(Holyhead)*.

10. Head towards Carmel Head but about halfway bear right to the chimney seen earlier. Some copper mining took place here.

11. Just before the chimney pick up a green track which passes below the second white tower. Go up to a stile at a gateway.

12. Follow the clear track to a stile beside a gate. Slant right to another stile and descend towards a coniferous plantation.

13. Pass a pool on the right. Join another track and bear left.

14. Continue on the track to the farm buildings of Mynachdy (6). Go through the gate ahead and continue to a stile.

15. Keep ahead over grass to another gate. Don't go through it but follow the fence to a ladder stile.

16. Continue on the track to a lane. Keep ahead and follow it for about 1 mile.

17. Pass a house called Fron Ddu and shortly turn left on a lane to the car park and start.

Facilities:

Small parking area where the footpath from Mynachdy joins the lane. Full facilities at Cemaes Bay.

Church Bay (Porth Swtan) – Mynydd y Garn – Ynys y Fydlyn – Church Bay (Porth Swtan)

OS Maps:	1:50 000 Landranger Sheet 114; 1:25 000 Pathfinder Sheet 733.
Start:	Lane end above Church Bay beach, G.R. 300892.
Access:	Church Bay *(Porth Swtan)* is signposted off the A5025 at Llanfaethlu and Llanrhyddlad. Some Holyhead-Amlwch buses pass through Rhydwyn, 1½ miles from Church Bay.
Parking:	Church Bay *(Porth Swtan)* car park.
Grade:	Strenuous – cliff and field paths, tracks and lanes.
Time:	4 hours.

Points of Interest:

1. The church in the name 'Church Bay' is St Rhuddlad's Church – its spire is a local landmark. 'Swtan' is an old Welsh name for whiting, a fish landed here. The beach is sandy and sheltered by rocks of Pre-Cambrian origin. Watch out for the rare chough and the more common oystercatcher. On warm, sunny days lizards may be seen sunning themselves on rocks close to the path. Butterflies such as the common blue and peacock visit the cliff top flowers.

2. From Mynydd y Garn there are good views of the nearby coast and islands – Church Bay, Carmel Head, Cemlyn Bay, West Mouse, The Skerries and, to the south, Holyhead Mountain. Below the hill, on the eastern side, lies the small village of Llanfairynghornwy. A semaphore station was sited on the south-east slope of Mynydd y Garn at the farmhouse of Craig y Gwynt. This was the Cefn Du telegraph station built by the Trustees of Liverpool Docks in 1841. The most westerly station was on Holyhead Mountain and from there messages were sent via Cefn Du, Mynydd Eilian, Puffin Island, the Great Orme and Hilbre

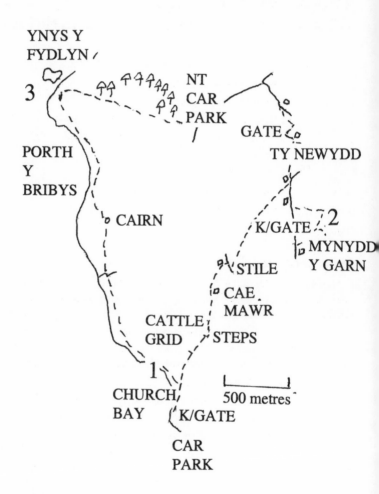

YNYS Y
FYDLYN

3

NT
CAR
PARK

PORTH
Y
BRIBYS

GATE

TY NEWYDD

CAIRN

K/GATE

2

MYNYDD
Y GARN

STILE

CAE
MAWR

CATTLE
GRID

STEPS

1

CHURCH
BAY

K/GATE

500 metres

CAR
PARK

Island to Liverpool. The usual time from Holyhead to Liverpool was 5 or 6 minutes. The monument on the summit of Mynydd y Garn is to William Thomas, a Sheriff of Anglesey, who became a ship owner. The rare chough – a black bird with red legs and red beak – may be seen flying in this area and on the western cliffs. They are usually in pairs.

3. This is a delightful, secluded spot with a shingle beach, backdrop of forest, steep cliffs and a rugged island, Ynys y Fydlyn. The lake between the island and the forest has now silted up and pheasants live in the wood awaiting the winter shoot. A permissive path, only open February to mid-September, goes north along the cliffs to National Trust land near Carmel Head. Close to Ynys y Fydlyn, the Swedish barque, Hudiksvall, lies in pieces under the waves. On her way from Liverpool to New York in 1890, she was forced into the bay to shelter from strong winds, and she foundered on the rocks. By the time the Holyhead lifeboat came to the rescue, the anchors had gone and she was on her beam end and breaking up. The crew had lashed themselves to the upper rails. After a rope was fixed the crew was able to reach the lifeboat and all were saved.

Walk Directions: (-) denotes Point of Interest

1. Above the beach (1) turn right onto an enclosed path above the bay. Enter a field and follow the left edge.

2. After passing through a gap into the next field, slant right to the far corner. Pass a ruin and keep uphill slanting right to a stile in the right-hand wall.

3. At a track turn left. Ignore a left fork and continue uphill. Where the track bends left to a cattle grid, turn right a few paces to a footpath signpost and steps.

4. Bear left across the field to the corner of a wall and cross into a field. Follow the right edge to the corner and cross steps into the next field.

5. Keep ahead through the middle of the field to a stile. Now slant left passing hedges and farm buildings on the right. Join a track and follow

it through a gate to reach a lane.

6. Turn right and, in a few metres, opposite the track to Cae-Mawr, turn left over a stile. Follow the right edge of the field.

7. Towards the end of the field bear left slightly to a low marker post. Keep ahead to reach a track and follow it to a lane.

8. Turn right and, shortly, ignore a stile on the left (it is used on the return). Continue on the lane to a kissing-gate on the left.

9. Go through the field to a gap in the left corner. After passing through a kissing-gate bear right uphill on a stepped path to the summit of Mynydd y Garn (2).

10. Return to the lower path at the kissing-gate. Turn right, with a wall on the left. Cross a stile, go through a kissing-gate and at the next field keep ahead to a wall corner.

11. Cross the wall and follow the left boundary down to the lane. The stile is rather hidden and is a few paces left of a gate.

12. Turn right, passing the track used earlier. In another 100 metres, just past a house on the left, take a wide path on the left through gorse and heather.

13. Cross a drive and continue downhill to reach another track. Bear right and pass a house called Ty Newydd. After passing the house go through a gate on the right.

14. Keep ahead a few metres and look for a rough stile on the left. Cross to another stile and keep ahead across a narrow field to a stone stile. Follow the left edge of a field, alongside gorse, downhill to an open field. Turn right, bearing right again to a stone stile.

15. Turn left on the lane. Ignore a dead end lane on the right. In another 800 metres, at a point where the lane bends left, turn right onto a track.

16. Pass through a National Trust car park (Mynachdy) and go through a kissing-gate. Follow the track that goes alongside a forest and descend to the cove at Ynys y Fydlyn (3).

17. Take a path on the left up to a stile and follow the path – narrow in places – along the side of the cliffs to Porth y Bribys.

18. Continue on the coast path and go up to a cairn. The route is away from the cliffs at this point. Continue through fields well marked by stiles.

19. After crossing a stream the path returns to the cliffs. Continue over a stile and where there is a banking and fields on the left look for a path lower down the slope. It goes through gorse to a stile.

20. Continue above the cliffs. At a corner keep ahead through a field to join the outward route. Retrace your steps to the start.

Facilities:

Small car park where the track for Ynys y Fydlyn leaves the lane. Toilets in Church Bay car park. Cafe nearby, cold drinks, ice cream. Refreshments also at The Lobster Pot and Church Bay Inn.

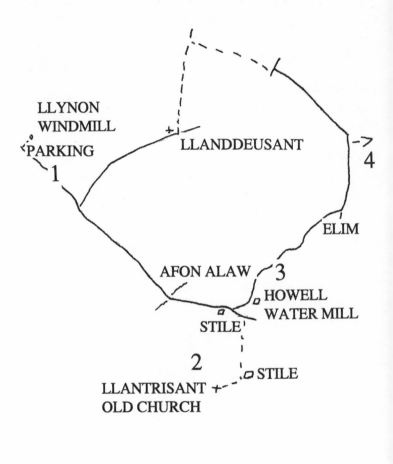

LLYNON
WINDMILL
PARKING
1

LLANDDEUSANT

4

ELIM

AFON ALAW   3

HOWELL
WATER MILL

STILE

STILE

2

LLANTRISANT
OLD CHURCH

500 metres

Llynon Mill (Melin Llynon) – Llantrisant Old Church – Howell Mill – Elim – Llanddeusant – Llynon Mill (Melin Llynon)

OS Maps:	1:50 000 Landranger Sheet 114; 1:25 000 Pathfinder Sheet 734.
Start:	Llynon Mill, G.R. 340852.
Access:	Llanddeusant can be reached from the B5109, west of Trefor, and from the A5025, south of Llanfaethlu. Follow signs for the mill. Two buses each day from Amlwch and Holyhead pass through Llanddeusant..
Parking:	Car park at Llynon Mill.
Grade:	Easy – Field paths, tracks and lanes.
Time:	2 hours.

Points of Interest:

1. After 60 years of disuse the Llynon Mill was finally restored and opened to the public in 1984. At one time there were more than 150 windmills in Wales, many of them on Anglesey, an ideal place to utilize wind power.

The first windmills were the post-mills. The whole mill structure, a wooden box on posts, could be turned to face the wind. Sails drove millstones but they were dangerous and could not be controlled. By the 16th century the round, straight-sided, stone tower mills had taken over. With the aid of a pole, their caps (tops) could be rotated to move the sails into the wind. About 200 years later, the towers became tapering and taller, raising the cap and sails to catch more wind. In Anglesey, the Penmon and Benllech quarries produced good quality mill-stones. Llynon Mill was built in 1776 and the first miller, Thomas

Jones, was 90 when he died. The tenancy passed to his descendants but the repeal of the Corn Laws in 1846 led to a decline in the use of windmills and this mill became disused by 1923. Storms damaged the cap allowing water to enter the mill. Anglesey Borough Council purchased Llynon Mill in 1978 and restoration was carried out by specialist millwrights from Lincolnshire.

2. Llantrisant Old Church is at present looked after by the Friends of Friendless Churches. Built in the 14th century it is dedicated to St Afran, St Ieuan and St Sannan. The south chapel was added later in the 17th century. The church has some interesting 17th and 18th century memorials and 19th century box pews.

3. In the Middle Ages there were over 60 mills on Anglesey including one here close to the River Alaw. The early mills would have been quite small, consisting of a water wheel driving a set of stones, some storage space and a place to dry grain. The present mill, Howell Mill, was enlarged in 1850 on the upstream side. Restoration work was carried out about 100 years later and the mill won a conservation award. The leat is fed by a dammed section of the River Alaw upstream which forms a small reservoir. This mill has survived but most water mills closed when it was realised that windmills provided a more reliable source of energy on Anglesey. Watermills require a constant supply of water, which could not be guaranteed in dry summers.

4. The barrow, Bedd Branwen, is traditionally associated with Branwen, daughter of Llyr, whose story is told in the collection of classical Welsh tales known as the Mabinogion. In the story Branwen marries Matholwch, King of Ireland, and the wedding feast is celebrated at Aberffraw. Her half-brother Efnisien is angry when he finds out that Branwen has married without his consent and he mutilates Matholwch's horses. Branwen and her husband sail to Ireland but, because of the insult, she is soon forced to work in the kitchen. She rears a starling, teaches it to speak, and after three years sends the bird to Wales with news of her misery. Her brother Bendigeidfran sails to Ireland and in the ensuing battle only 7 men from the 'Island of the Mighty' (Britain) survive. Branwen and the 7

return home with the head of Bendigeidfran. They land on the west coast of Anglesey and as they sit and rest, Branwen looks towards Ireland and the Island of the Mighty. Because of the trouble she has caused, she regrets being born. On the bank of the Alaw she dies of a broken heart and they bury her there. The Mabinogion was written in the 11th century – Aberffraw was then the chief court of the Princes of Gwynedd. However, the story may include an earlier oral tradition.

Excavation has revealed that the barrow was built in the Bronze Age as a communal burial place. At the centre there is a large stone which may have been a monument long beforehand. An urn with bones was found early in the 19th century. When full excavation took place about 30 years ago several urns containing cremated bones and imported beads were uncovered. The site appears to have been used at different periods with two sets of burials. Beside some of the urns there were accessory pots (smaller pots) containing ear bones of newborn babies, suggestive of some kind of ritual. To reach the site follow the track across a cattle grid. Shortly before the track bends left at some woods, there is a field gate on the right. Although the land is private, if the land is not being used for crops or hay, access is usually allowed to the monument. Slant right across the field for some distance. The low barrow with its central stone is in a bend of the River Alaw.

Walk Directions: (-) denotes Point of Interest

1. Starting from the car park at Llynon Mill (1) turn left on the lane. At the crossroads keep ahead on the lane signposted Trefor.

2. The lane crosses the River Alaw and passes a house on the right called New Hafren. Look for a narrow lane on the left. This is taken after visiting Llantrisant old church.

3. To visit the church, continue 100 metres to a stone stile on the right. Follow the right edge of the field, keep ahead through a gate and pass a farm on the left. Cross a stile in the left corner and turn right through a gate to the church (2).

4. From the church return the same way to the lane. Turn left then right on the narrow lane seen earlier. Follow it to Howell Mill (3).

5. With the mill on the right, follow the rough lane uphill. It bends right to a wider lane at Elim.

6. Turn left for about 400 metres to a track on the right for Glan Alaw. Bedd Branwen lies in a field off this track (4).

7. Continue on the lane. The lane bends left past houses to a junction. Cross the road directly to a track.

8. Follow the track and where it bends right go through the second of two gates on the left. Follow the wall and hedge on the left. Cross a rough stile into the next field.

9. Continue to a stile on the left of the church ahead. Follow an enclosed path to the road in Llanddeusant village.

10. Turn right and at the crossroads turn right again to the start at Llynon Mill.

Facilities:

Tea-room and toilets at Llynon Mill. The mill is open April to September. Closed on Mondays.

Breakwater Country Park – Holyhead Mountain (Mynydd Twr) – South Stack – North Stack – Breakwater Country Park

OS Maps: 1:50 000 Landranger Sheet 114;
               1:25 000 Pathfinder Sheet 734.

Start: Breakwater Country Park, G.R.227833.

Access: From the A5 in Holyhead take the road signposted Marina and Breakwater Country Park. At the marina turn left to the country park. Trains to Holyhead. Buses from Bangor and many places on Anglesey to Holyhead, 1½ miles from the start.

Parking: Breakwater Country Park.

Grade: Strenuous – cliffs and hill paths. Track and short stretch of lane.

Time: 4 hours.

Points of Interest:

1. Officially opened in 1994, the Breakwater Country Park consists of quarry floor, farmland, coast, heath and mountain. About 7 million tons of stone was taken from the Breakwater Quarry to build the Holyhead Breakwater, which was finished in 1873. At one time 1500 men were employed on the construction, working shifts day and night in a dangerous environment – 51 men lost their lives over an eight year period. A broad gauge railway with several lines was built between the quarries and the breakwater site to carry the stone. The tall chimney was built about 1901 for the use of a brickworks plant here. It used both round and square kilns.

2. The summit of Holyhead Mountain (Mynydd Twr) provided a place of refuge for Iron Age people during times of Irish invasion. They built a hillfort here, Caer y Twr, covering 17 acres. On the steep SE

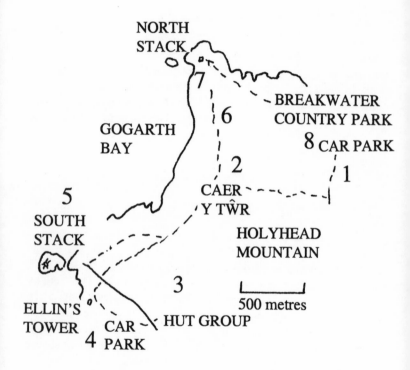

NORTH
STACK

BREAKWATER
COUNTRY PARK

8 CAR PARK

1

GOGARTH
BAY

7

6

2

CAER
Y TŴR

5
SOUTH
STACK

HOLYHEAD
MOUNTAIN

3

ELLIN'S
TOWER

4 CAR
PARK

HUT GROUP

500 metres

and SW slopes no additional defences were necessary but around the northern sides a high wall was built. The entrance was in the NE corner. The fort was still being used during the Roman occupation and the base of a Roman watchtower is close to the trig point. Coins dating 4th century AD have been found here. The views from the summit are spectacular, the panorama covering Holy Island *(Ynys Gybi)*, much of western Anglesey and the distant mountains of Snowdonia.

3. Over 50 huts were found on the Ty Mawr site in the mid 19th century when the settlement was partly excavated by William Stanley, a local landowner. Less than half are evident now but those that remain are in a good state of preservation. Ten are large round huts and their walls were probably the same height as they are today. On these wooden posts were placed and covered with straw or reeds to form a high conical roof. The round huts were the living quarters while the small rectangular huts were workshops. Next to the huts were small ploughed fields. The site has been in use from the Neolithic period to later than the Roman era.

4. Ellin's tower was built in the 19th century as a summerhouse for Ellin, wife of Lord Stanley. It is now a RSPB visitor centre. Binoculars and telescopes are provided for viewing the nearby seabird colony where, in late spring and early summer, guillemots, razorbills and puffins nest on the cliffs. Other birds to look for in the reserve, which covers Holyhead Mountain and the cliffs between the Stacks, are raven, chough and peregrine. In spring and summer the cliffs are a mass of colour from the flowers of thrift, spring squill, sea campion, sheep's bit, stonecrop and restharrow.

5. The South Stack suspension bridge to the island is now open to visitors during the spring and summer months. The lighthouse was built in 1809 and a few years ago became automatic. Note the folds in the rock face. The barque Primrose Hill wrecked south of here in 1900 on her way from Liverpool to Australia. Caught in a north-west gale, her sails torn and with her anchors dragging, she struck submerged rocks and broke up with the loss of 33 lives. The only survivor was aloft when the ship rolled over and he dropped on to the top of the cliff.

6. This is the site of a former semaphore station. Built in the early 19th century it was the first in a chain of stations linking Holyhead to Liverpool. Two vertical columns carried two pairs of arms each which could be set in various elevations to transmit numerical codes. The system was extremely efficient but it was soon taken over by electric telegraph, which later had a station here.

7. The fog station at North Stack started operating in 1857. The keepers used donkeys to carry their food and the explosives for the fog warning gun. One donkey called Neddy, who lived to the age of 24, was buried at North Stack. A fog warning gun, which is now in the country park, was recovered from the bottom of the cliffs in 1984 and floated to Holyhead Harbour. It had been thrown into the sea some years previously after becoming redundant on the arrival of electricity at North Stack.

8. The memorial is to missing airmen. Only two survived of the 10 men crew who bailed out of the American aircraft on 22 December, 1944. After a wartime sortie the B-24J Liberator, codenamed Jigs Up, should have landed at Cheddington but, because of fog it was diverted to Atcham, another American airbase. Bad weather had closed Atcham airfield forcing the Jigs Up and two other aircraft to fly to RAF Valley on Anglesey. Over North Wales the Jigs Up ran into navigational problems when its G-Box broke down. Visibility was poor, the pilot lost radio contact with the ground and all the B-24s were running out of fuel while having to wait for other aircraft to land. The Jigs Up informed the accompanying B-24s that two of its engines were failing and the crew were standing by to bail out. The other two aircraft landed safely. However, the crew of the Jigs Up seem to have jumped prematurely as they were missing when the final order was given to bail out. The pilot and co-pilot parachuted to land near Holyhead and moments later the pilotless Liberator crashed into the headland at North Stack. It is assumed that the missing eight jumped over the Irish Sea. Despite an extensive search they were not picked up. In June 1992 divers located the aircraft debris and brought up a propeller blade which has been restored and mounted on the stone plinth. The following April the memorial was unveiled at a service of dedication.

Another salvaged propeller blade was presented to members of the missing crew's families and this has been made into a similar memorial in North Carolina.

Walk Directions: (-) denotes Point of Interest

1. Starting from the car park (1) turn left past the chimney and pool. Turn right into a quarry.

2. In a few paces bear right on a path which rises above the quarry. It bends left to some houses.

3. Pass a house called Fron Cottage and before a footpath signpost on the left, turn right on a track. Continue on a path, uphill.

4. Ignore a path on the left and keep ahead past small fields. The path slants right and bends left to the trig point on top of Holyhead Mountain (Mynydd Twr) (2).

5. Take a path going north and bear left to meet a path near an information board. Continue downhill to a wide path along the side of the mountain, above Gogarth Bay.

6. Bear left and ignore all side paths. Pass some 'dishes' and at a tarmac track turn left and follow it to a lane.

7. Turn left for about 600 metres. At a car park on the right, a stile on the left gives access to Ty Mawr hut group (3).

8. Return to the lane and cross to the car park. Take the first path on the right to Ellin's Tower (4).

9. From the tower ascend to the lane. Turn left towards South Stack (5).

10. Facing the gate to South Stack take a path on the right. It rises to a lookout and continues along a small ridge.

11. As it approaches the tarmac track used earlier fork right to meet the track. Retrace your route along the side of Holyead Mountain.

12. Pass the descent route off Holyhead Mountain. At a fork in the path go left to a small top (6).

13. Descend the steep path and bear right to join a track. Turn left to the fog station (7) above North Stack.

14. Just before the buildings turn right on a narrow path, and keep the sea on the left. When the path joins a track bear left and descend to a kissing-gate and memorial (8).

15. Bear right through more kissing-gates to the start at the country park.

Facilities:

Alternative parking at South Stack. Toilets in the country park and alongside the lane at South Stack. Refreshments at the South Stack Kitchen restaurant. Ice cream van near the cliffs in the summer. Ellin's tower is open Easter – mid September. Access to South Stack Easter – end September. Heritage trails in the Breakwater Country Park. Full facilities in Holyhead *(Caergybi)*.

Borthwen – Rhoscolyn Head – Porth Saint – Bwa Du – Borthwen

OS Maps:	1:50 000 Landranger Sheet 114; 1:25 000 Pathfinder Sheet 750.
Start:	Borthwen beach car park, Rhoscolyn, G.R. 273752.
Access:	Leave the A5 at Valley and take the B4545 to Four Mile Bridge. Turn left to Rhoscolyn and the beach. Buses from Holyhead to Rhoscolyn.
Parking:	Car park at Borthwen.
Grade:	Moderate – cliff and field paths, track and lane.
Time:	2½-3 hours.

Points of Interest:

1. Late in the 19th century, fishermen based in Rhoscolyn dredged oyster beds off the west coast of Anglesey and, for some years, oyster catching was a thriving industry in this small village. Nowadays, Rhoscolyn's sandy beach between headlands is popular with families.

2. St Gwenfaen founded a church near Rhoscolyn in the 6th century and this holy well is named after her. The water was thought to cure mental disorders and quartz stones were thrown in the well as an offering. Almost all the stonework lies below ground level and steps lead down into a chamber with corner seats, in front of the pool.

3. The Southern Cross sank off Rhoscolyn Head in March 1855 after striking a submerged rock in thick fog. Although her crew of 17 managed to escape in the ship's lifeboat, they were soon in trouble again when the boat struck another rock. They managed to scramble onto a large rock but were stranded 12 hours before rescue came in the form of Rhoscolyn's lifeboat. In 1901, while assisting the crew of the J.W. Wearing near Porth Saint the Rhoscolyn lifeboat and the schooner collided, smashing four oars. Another oar was driven into the

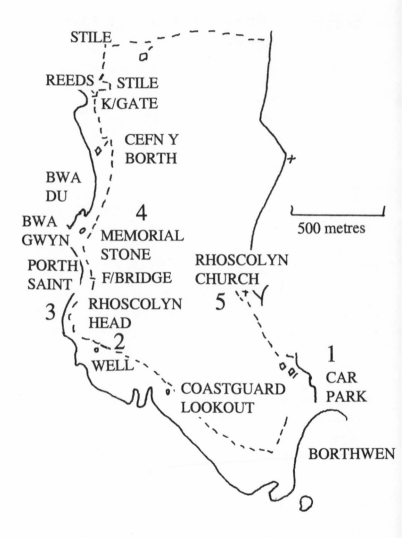

STILE

REEDS STILE
K/GATE

CEFN Y
BORTH

BWA
DU

BWA
GWYN

PORTH
SAINT

MEMORIAL
STONE

F/BRIDGE

4

3

RHOSCOLYN
HEAD

2

WELL

RHOSCOLYN
CHURCH

5

COASTGUARD
LOOKOUT

1
CAR
PARK

BORTHWEN

500 metres

lifeboat's side. George Smith severed it with an axe to get them under way. Some years later, when he was over 80, Smith himself was rescued by the lifeboat after spending 18 hours clinging to Rhoscolyn Beacon. He had been visiting his lobster pots when his boat smashed against the rocks in a sudden gale.

4. The seaward side of this small memorial stone bears a simple inscription: 'Tyger Sep 17th 1819'. It commemorates the sagacity and devotion of a dog who saved the lives of his master and two men and a boy. During a dense fog, their ship hit Maen Piscar, a treacherous rock about one kilometre offshore. The captain was unsure of his whereabouts but Tyger, his retriever, seemed to know the direction of the nearest land. He probably heard the echo of his barks bouncing off the cliffs. As the ketch sank, the dog jumped into the sea and the captain, having faith in the dog's instinct, followed his direction. The captain, a strong swimmer, helped the two men, and the boy hung on to the dog's collar. After taking the boy to land, Tyger swam back to his master. One of the men was having difficulties and the dog took hold of his collar and pulled him to shore. Returning to the sea, he helped the other man and his master to the rocks. As they all lay exhausted, Tyger, his strength completely gone, gave his master one last lick, then died.

5. Rhoscolyn Church is dedicated to Saint Gwenfaen, daughter of Pawl Hen of the Isle of Man. The first church was here in AD 630 and the second, built about 800 years later, was destroyed by fire. The present 19th century church has the 15th century font and door. A tall memorial in the churchyard is in memory of the lifeboat coxswain, Owen Owens, and four others who lost their lives going to the aid of the steamship Timbo during a storm in December 1920. The 80 mph winds and huge waves were too much for the rowing boat to cope with and, as the Timbo was holding her anchors, the lifeboat crew turned back and made for the shelter of Llanddwyn. However, it took seven hours to reach there and during that time five of the lifeboatmen, including Owen Owens, were swept into the sea. Meanwhile, the crew in the Timbo launched one of their own boats only to lose four lives. The steamship eventually broke away from her anchors and, without

further loss of life, beached on the coast at Dinas Dinlle. The five lifeboatmen who drowned are buried together in Rhoscolyn churchyard.

Walk Directions: (-) denotes Point of Interest

1. Starting from the beach car park (1) walk back along the lane and in about 250 metres turn left through a kissing-gate.

2. Pass a house on the right and keep ahead to a stile. Follow the right edge of two fields and before the end of the second one turn left to a corner stile.

3. Follow the right edge of the field to a kissing-gate. Cross the field past enclosed wells to a wall corner. Go over a footbridge and stile and continue on an enclosed path. Bear right and left between gardens and cross a track to a stile.

4. Walk ahead and soon follow a wall on the right to a kissing-gate. Go uphill to the old coastguard lookout – a fine viewpoint of the coast and out to Rhoscolyn Beacon.

5. Continue on a clear path to St Gwenfaen's well (2).

6. Go through the kissing-gate ahead and follow a wall – take care on these cliffs – around Rhoscolyn Head (3). The path continues along the cliffs to an inlet and footbridge at Porth Saint.

7. Continue around the cliffs but soon bear right over open ground to reach the cliff edge again at the White Arch *(Bwa Gwyn)*. This was once the site of a china clay quarry.

8. Continue on a clear path and in about 100 metres look for a low isolated stone above the sea (4).

9. The path descends to a stile above an inlet at Black Arch *(Bwa Du)*. Marble quarried here was used in the building of Worcester, Peterborough and Bristol Cathedrals.

10. Continue ahead on a clear path through rocky outcrops. After two kissing-gates reach a stile at the drive exit of Cefn y Borth.

11. Turn left a few metres then bear right to a kissing-gate at a reedy area.

12. Follow the fence on the left to a corner. Stay with the fence a few more paces then slant right uphill to a field gate. Don't go through it but follow the wall on the left to a corner stile.

13. Cross a wettish area to a clear path and bear left. It soon bends sharp right and passes through a wall gap. Keep left and ignore a path going to a house. Go through another wall gap and follow a wall on the right to a stile.

14. Bear right here and pass rocks on the left. Reach an access track and follow it to a lane.

15. At the lane turn right. Pass a chapel and continue to Rhoscolyn Church (5).

16. Bear right to pass the church on the left. At the end of the churchyard wall turn left through a kissing-gate and follow the wall on the left to a stile.

17. Bear slightly left and cross a drive to a ladder stile. Cross the middle of the field to a kissing-gate in stone walls. Continue ahead to the next kissing-gate. Cross a track and follow the left edge of the field to a small gate.

18. Follow the path to a driveway and lane. Turn right to the start.

Facilities:

Parking space near the church. Toilets at the beach car park. Refreshments at Four Mile Bridge and Trearddur Bay. Several camp sites in the area. All facilities in Holyhead *(Caergybi)*.

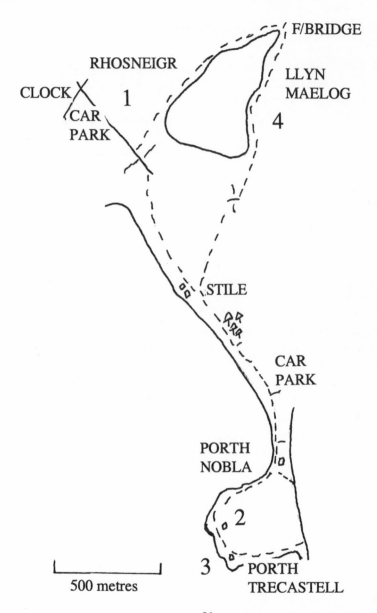

RHOSNEIGR

CLOCK

CAR PARK

1

F/BRIDGE

LLYN MAELOG

4

STILE

CAR PARK

PORTH NOBLA

2

3

PORTH TRECASTELL

500 metres

Rhosneigr – Tywyn Fferam
–Porth Nobla – Barclodiad y Gawres
– Llyn Maelog – Rhosneigr

OS Maps:	1:50 000 Landranger Sheet 114;
	1:25 000 Pathfinder Sheet 750.
Start:	Rhosneigr crossroads and clock, G.R. 318731.
Access:	Rhosneigr is on the A4080, reached from the A5 1½ miles west of Gwalchmai. Trains from Holyhead and Bangor. Buses from Holyhead and Llangefni.
Parking:	Rhosneigr car park, near the library.
Grade:	Easy – mainly dune, cliff and lakeside paths.
Time:	2½ hours.

Points of Interest:

1. Nowadays, Rhosneigr is a peaceful, family resort. Back in the 18th century, the area was known for its evil villains, the Robbers of Crigyll *(Lladron Crigyll)*. Ships frequently wrecked on the treacherous rocks near the Crigyll estuary and the robbers plundered them. They were rarely caught. When the Liverpool brigantine, Loveday and Betty came ashore in a gale, the captain went for assistance. On his return he found the vessel stripped of everything, including the sails. Crew and passengers sometimes drowned while robbers looted cargo and such depredations carried on into the 19th century.

By 1872 Rhosneigr had a lifeboat and in 1876 ten men were saved from the Clifton which had foundered on the Crigyll reef. Two years later, a Dutch brigantine, the Elisabeth Klousterboer came to grief on the same rocks. Earlier, the coastguard had tried to warn ships off the rocks by sending up rockets. He warned off two vessels but it was too late for the Dutch vessel. The lifeboat found only one survivor. The wreck of the clipper Norman Court lies north of Rhosneigr, off *(Traeth)* Cymyran Beach. She was carrying sugar from Java in March 1883 when she hit rocks. Her mast collapsed and with the sea breaking over her, the crew clung to the fore-rigging. Rhoscolyn lifeboat was not available and the Rhosneigr lifeboatmen had to row against the wind. Despite two gallant attempts they could not quite make it. An appeal was made to Holyhead and their lifeboat crew came to Rhosneigr by special train to launch the boat. This attempt was successful and all survivors were saved. The coxswain Edward Jones received the RNLI silver medal.

2. The ruined cairn on Mynydd Bach once had a diameter of 40 feet with a grave in the centre. When it was excavated about 1953 only one piece of pottery was found, indicating that the site had been disturbed previously. It is probably a Beaker period burial place.

3. Barclodiad y Gawres is a partly restored Neolithic cruciform passage grave covered by a circular mound of stones and earth. The name means 'the apronful of the giantess'. Similar graves are to be found in the Boyne valley in Ireland. It has a long passage which leads to a dome shaped central area and side chambers. The most interesting feature of the grave must be the decorated stones – five have patterns of zigzags, lozenges and spirals. At the end of the passage there are two of these stones on the left and one on the right. The others are in the left and right side chambers. During excavations (1952-3) the burnt bones of two men were found in the grave. A funerary ritual had taken place in the central area. A funerary ritual had taken place in the central area. A fire had been lit and then quenched with a strange stew before being completely covered with limpet shells and pebbles. The weird concoction consisted of frog, toad, natterjack, grass snake, hare, shrew, mouse, eel, whiting and wrasse, all recognisable by their bones.

4. Llyn Maelog, a natural lake, used to be tidal until sand separated it from the sea. Fringed with reeds, it is a haven for birds. In summer look for little grebe, great crested grebe, tufted duck, ruddy duck, pochard, shelduck, greylag goose and swans. The reedbeds attract sedge warbler, whitethroat and reed bunting. Plants to look for include white water-lilies, water milfoil and the tall pink flowering rush. Water

forget-me-not and yellow loosestrife grow in damp places near the lake.

Walk Directions: (-) denotes Point of Interest

1. From the clock at Rhosneigr crossroads take the road *(Ffordd Maelog)* past the garage.

2. Cross a bridge and turn right on a path into the dunes. Keep a building on the left and continue on a clear path to reach a track at some houses.

3. Cross the track and a ladder stile. Pass some trees, cross a footbridge, go directly over a grass track. Continue to a car park on Tywyn Fferam.

4. Cross the car park to the far right corner. Take the path through the dunes.

5. The path bends left to the road. Turn right for 200 metres to a footpath sign on the right. Alternatively, follow the beach and join the headland path at the end of Porth Nobla.

6. Follow the path around the headland. The remains of a cairn (2) can be seen on the left of the path just before the descent to a footbridge. Climb up to Barclodiad y Gawres burial chamber (3).

7. Continue on the path to reach the road at Porth Trecastell.

8. Turn left on the road. Retrace your steps on the dune path – or follow the beach – to the track at the houses.

9. Bear right along the track to the road. Turn right and after crossing a bridge go left on a track.

10. Keep ahead, the track becomes grass. Go through a kissing-gate and cross open land beside Llyn Maelog (4). Continue over stiles to the end of the lake.

11. Cross a footbridge and pass below a disused quarry. Follow the path close to the lake and pass a conservation area. Continue through kissing-gates to the road.

12. Turn right to the start at the crossroads.

Facilities:

Toilets in the car park. Car park and portaloos at Tywyn Fferam. Enquire at the Llys Llywelyn Coastal Heritage Centre in Aberffraw for the key to Barclodiad y Gawres. Refreshments in Rhosneigr. Campsite nearby.

Aberffraw – Afon Ffraw – Porth Cwyfan – Llangwyfanisaf – Aberffraw

OS Maps:	1:50 000 Landranger Sheet 114; 1:25 000 Pathfinder Sheet 768.
Start:	Aberffraw, east side of the old bridge across the Afon Ffraw, G.R. 356689.
Access:	Take the A4080 from Menai Bridge (Porthaethwy). Aberffraw is 6 miles west of Newborough (Niwbwrch). Just before Aberffraw turn left on a minor road. Buses from Bangor, Llangefni and Holyhead.
Parking:	Aberffraw, parking space on the east side of the old bridge.
Grade:	Moderate – cliff and field paths, beach, tracks and lane.
Time:	3 hours.

Points of Interest:

1. Aberffraw was the main court of the Princes of Gwynedd from the 6th – 13th centuries and from here they ruled all of North Wales. Nothing remains of the timber palace although it survived Edward I's invasion. Later, in 1317 it was demolished and used in the construction of Caernarfon Castle. The court *(llys)* was probably situated in the older part of Aberffraw village. Excavation west of Bodorgan Square revealed ditches and banks constructed 1st-14th centuries A.D. The earlier ditches belonged to a Roman fort while a non-Roman rampart was 5th-13th century. Finds included pieces of Roman and 13th century pottery. Maelgwn Gwynedd probably had a royal court here in the 6th century. A Christian ruler, he gave St Cybi land at Holyhead and St Seiriol land at Penmon. Rhodri Mawr ruled most of Wales from Aberffraw AD 844-878 when he inherited Powys and married into Ceredigion. By the 12th and 13th centuries the court of Aberffraw was

involved with political and economic affairs beyond Wales. The last Prince of Aberffraw was Llywelyn ap Gruffudd, Llywelyn the Last, who was killed in 1282.

2. At the far end of the headland, on the eastern side, some stones may be seen protruding above the grass. These are the remains of a burial cairn of about 25 feet diameter, built here 2-3000 BC. This spot is also a Mesolithic site – 7000 BC. It was excavated about 1974 uncovering many pieces of flint and chert. Some had been made into arrow tips and scrapers. Finds included two small axes which may have been used for cutting down trees. No bones were present but they would not have survived in the sandy soil. Some burnt hazelnut shells were found in a pit. In 7000 BC the sea level was lower than now, and the site was some distance from the sea, overlooking a river valley. The windblown sand dunes across the river have more recently filled in a large estuary, putting an end to Aberffraw's small port and shipyard. Today, from the promontory there are lovely views across Caernarfon Bay to the hills of the Lleyn *(Llyn)* Peninsula.

3. The tiny church of St Cwyfan was founded in the 7th century and rebuilt in stone in the 12th century. Since then it has been added to and restored but most of the church is 14th century. The churchyard wall, which surrounds the island, was built during the 19th century to check erosion. Watch for the incoming tide as the causeway to the island is covered at high tide.

Walk Directions: (-) denotes Point of Interest

1. Starting from the car parking area on the east side of Aberffraw (1) cross the old bridge, which was built in 1731. Turn left along a track beside the river.

2. Where the track ends, take the coastal path behind a house. Turn left on an enclosed path that continues along the top of a wall.

3. The path descends to the Afon Ffraw. Pass a white cottage and ignore a track on the right. Continue to a kissing-gate.

4. Bear left to the end of the headland (2). Continue around the coast above rocks and a sandy beach. Go through a kissing-gate and down steps to a shingle beach.

5. Ignore a path on the right. Continue about another 150 metres to a path at the back of the rocks.

6. Continue above low cliffs and over a number of stiles. Seals may be seen in the shallow waters or basking on small islands. In about 1¼ miles the path reaches the beach of Porth Cwyfan.

7. Continue around the top of the beach and follow the causeway to the tiny church on the island (3).

8. Return along the causeway and take a track that bears left uphill past a white cottage called Tyntwll.

9. In about 800 metres the track descends and bears sharp left at trees near a house called Llangwyfanisaf. At this bend turn right to cross the fence at a point where it has wooden bars.

10. Bear right across the middle of the field to a kissing-gate beside a broad gate. Maintain the same direction to a kissing-gate at a footbridge.

11. Follow the left-hand wall and enter another field through a kissing-gate. Bear slightly left to a narrow gate at a footbridge. Slant left to a kissing-gate and follow the left edge of the field to a lane.

12. Turn left and descend past St Beuno's Church to Aberffraw village. Bear right in the square to return to the old bridge and starting point.

Facilities:

Tea-room and toilets at the Coastal Heritage Centre, Llys Llywelyn in Aberffraw. Two pubs in the village. Ice cream van near the bridge during the summer months. Exhibitions and information at the heritage centre, open April to September.

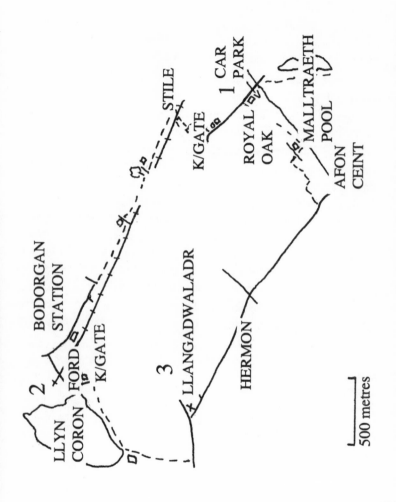

500 metres

Malltraeth – Llyn Coron – Llangadwaladr – Cefni Estuary – Malltraeth

OS Maps:	1:50 000 Landranger Sheet 114; 1:25 000 Pathfinder Sheet 750, 768.
Start:	Malltraeth, bridge over the Afon Cefni, G.R. 407687.
Access:	From Menai Bridge (Porthaethwy) take the A4080. Malltraeth is 2½ miles beyond Newborough (Niwbwrch). Buses from Bangor and Llangefni. Trains to Bodorgan Station from Bangor and Holyhead.
Parking:	Small parking area on the north-west side of the bridge.
Grade:	Moderate – paths, track, lane and road.
Time:	3 hours.

Points of Interest:

1. Malltraeth used to be called Malltraeth Yard because of the boatyard once here. Before the reclamation of the land, the estuary stretched almost to the A5 and the Afon Cefni was navigable as far as the quay at Llangefni. Coalmining took place on Malltraeth Marsh for several centuries. Early in the 19th century, the building of the high embankment, the 'Cob', changed part of the marsh into farmland. About the same time, a section of the Afon Cefni was canalised. Situated between the A4080 and the Cob, Malltraeth Pool is a haven for birds and in summer, heron, mute swan, shoveller, tufted duck, moorhen and coot may be seen here. High tide is the best time to watch waders in the estuary. Charles Tunnicliffe, the famous wildlife artist, spent the last 30 years of his life in Malltraeth where his studio looked out on the estuary.

2. Llyn Coron was once part of an estuary until the sand dunes at Aberffraw separated the lake from the open sea. The Afon Ffraw drains from the north-western side of this natural lake. Llyn Coron is

excellent for bird-watching, especially in winter when large numbers of ducks may be present. Great crested grebe, little grebe, mute swan, ruddy duck and coot may be seen all year. Listen for the evocative call of the curlew. Plants to look for include water-lilies, yellow loosestrife, water forget-me-not and marsh speedwell.

3. Cadwaladr was the son of Cadwallon who was the son of King Cadfan. The church, founded in the 7th century, was the burial ground for the court at Aberffraw. The early church was probably a wooden building while this present church dates from the 12th century. It contains the most important gravestone on Anglesey, the Cadfan stone. It has a Latin inscription which describes Cadfan as the 'wisest and most renowned of kings'. At one time the stone was used as a lintel for the south door. Saint Cadwaladr is commemorated in the 15th century east window. The Meyrick chapel, the north chapel, was added to the chancel and nave about 1640 and 90 years later a vault was built underneath it. There is a story of a macabre find in the vault when it was opened for a family burial in 1742. A strange coffin was standing upright and when opened it contained a man's body in fine clothing. Stained scratches on the inside of the coffin lid were proof that the man had been incarcerated alive. Nobody knew his identity. On the outside of the church there are some amusing gargoyles on the eastern gable.

Walk Directions: (-) denotes Point of Interest

1. Starting from the bridge (1) walk through the village of Malltraeth. Pass the Royal Oak on the left.

2. In another 200 metres, at houses and just before the road bends left, turn right through a kissing-gate onto an enclosed path. Continue by the left edge of a field and in the next field bear left and follow a wall to a ladder stile.

3. Bear right past buildings to a gate. Keep ahead by the left edge of the field to a stile in the corner. Turn left to the next stile and an access lane.

4. Turn right over a railway bridge and immediately cross a stile on the left. Keep to the left and continue over stiles. Pass the garden wall of a

house on the right and cross a stile onto a track.

5. Cross the track and take a path through woodland. Go through a kissing-gate and keep ahead through trees. At open ground, opposite a house, bear right to a ladder stile and road.

6. Turn left and in a few paces turn right through a kissing-gate. Follow a clear path until it reaches a road.

7. Keep ahead and where the road bends left continue on a lane. Pass Bodorgan Station on the left and continue on the lane to where it bends right.

8. Bear left on a track unsuitable for motor vehicles. Ignore a footpath on the right and continue over a bridge next to a ford. Pass a farmhouse on the left and turn right through a kissing-gate.

9. Follow the left edge of two fields to a stile and footbridge. Continue over damp ground and stay fairly close to the left wall. At the next fence go through a kissing-gate in the left corner.

10. Continue beside Llyn Coron (2). Cross a stile and bear left to a track. Go left past a cottage to the stile ahead.

11. Go through the field to a stile in the right-hand corner. Follow the right edge of the next field to the road.

12. Turn left and follow the road to Llangadwaladr. Ignore a lane on the left. In another 200 metres a track on the left leads to the Parish Church of St Cadwaladr (3).

13. Return to the road and follow the grass verge to Hermon. At the end of the village, and where the road bends left, keep ahead on a narrow lane.

14. Follow the lane for about a kilometre to where it forks at a high wall. To visit the Cefni Estuary, continue downhill to the shore.

15. Return to the fork and follow the metalled track. Pass a house and gardens on the right. At a gate turn right through a kissing-gate onto an enclosed path.

16. Continue to a fork in the path and keep left. Ignore a stile on the left but follow the path as it bears right to a lane.

17. Cross the lane to a path between houses. At the end of the gardens ignore the steps. Bear left and shortly follow a fence on the left.

18. At some reeds go through a kissing-gate. Follow the path to the road near the Royal Oak. Turn right to the starting point.

Facilities:

Picnic tables at the parking area. Two pubs in Malltraeth. Camp site nearby.

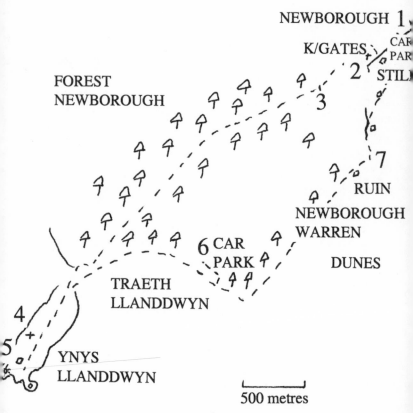

NEWBOROUGH 1

K/GATES 2 CAR PAR

STIL

FOREST NEWBOROUGH

3

7

RUIN

NEWBOROUGH WARREN

6 CAR PARK

DUNES

TRAETH LLANDDWYN

4

5

YNYS LLANDDWYN

500 metres

Newborough (Niwbwrch) – Newborough Forest – Ynys Llanddwyn – Traeth Llanddwyn – Newborough (Niwbwrch)

OS Maps:	1:50 000 Landranger Sheet 114; 1:25 000 Pathfinder Sheet 768.
Start:	Newborough car park, G.R. 423656.
Access:	Take the A4080 from Menai Bridge (Porthaethwy). At the crossroads in Newborough take the lane to Traeth Llanddwyn for about 150 metres. Buses from Bangor and Llangefni.
Parking:	Small car park in Newborough.
Grade:	Moderate – field, island and dune paths, forest track, beach and lane.
Time:	4-4½ hours.

Points of Interest:

1. Newborough *(Niwbwrch)* was settled about 1295 by the villagers of Llanfaes, who were evicted by Edward I when he built Beaumaris Castle. It became a bustling little town well known for its markets and fairs. The clearance of trees and the high winds caused sand to encroach on agricultural land and by the time of Elizabeth I, marram grass was planted to stabilize the dunes. Weaving the grass soon became a local cottage industry. The marram grass was harvested between August and November. After cutting it was heaped in the shape of a pyramid and left to ripen for a few weeks until nearly white. It was then steeped in water to make it supple and woven into plaits, usually of 11 strands. The plaits were made into mats, ropes, baskets and other goods. Some uses of mats were floor coverings, kneel mats, coverings for seed frames and box bed covers. The grass was also used

for fishermen's nets, brooms and as a filter in the copper mines. This local industry came to an end at the beginning of the 20th century.

2. Excavation has uncovered the foundation of a medieval court *(llys)*, one of several small courts on Anglesey where the Princes of Aberffraw would have stayed while travelling around the island. On these journeys they collected rent from tenants and held law courts. Centuries of sand covered the base of a hall and another building. Masonry is several courses high in places. Finds include pottery of the 13th and 14th centuries.

3. After being taken over by the Forestry Commission in 1946, this area of sand dunes was stabilized by the planting of Corsican pine. Other coniferous trees in the forest are lodgepole pine, Monterey pine and Scots pine. There are a few broadleaved trees such as oak, silver birch, elder and willow. A colourful medley of flowers grow alongside the track – evening primrose, heartsease pansy, common restharrow, viper's bugloss and orchids. Birds in the forest include goldcrest, siskin, redpoll and crossbill. Look out for red squirrels. About 80 years ago, many fragments of pottery dating 1600-1400 BC were found west of this track. Other finds were shell mounds, fossilized bones, flint arrowheads, scrapers and stone axes.

4. The ruins are the remains of a 16th century church dedicated to St Dwynwen, the patron saint of Welsh lovers. Only parts of the chancel stand above foundation level. Dwynwen lived in the 5th century and, after an unhappy love affair, she retreated to this island and devoted her life to God. She built a small chapel on the spot where the ruins are now. When she was dying she asked to see the sunset for the last time and was carried to the nearby cleft rock, north-west of the ruins. After her death, lovers made pilgrimages to her shrine and her holy well below the cleft rock. A sacred fish lived in the bottom of the well, a fresh water spring. Pilgrims would place a piece of cloth on the water and if the fish moved it, this was a sign the love was untrue. St Dwynwen's Day is the 25th January.

5. Early in the 19th century, Caernarfon harbour trustees built two pilot's cottages here and the navigational beacon which is below on the left. About 1845 they added two more cottages and the taller tower

which was soon converted into a lighthouse. The stones of St Dwynwen's church were probably used for the building of the cottages and towers. The pilots took turns in guiding ships into Caernarfon harbour and manning the lighthouse. Llanddwyn received its first functional lifeboat in 1840 and the cannon was used to alert the volunteer crew across the sand dunes in Newborough. The cannon was first used in 1841 when a Liverpool ship, the Mountaineer, foundered on a sand bar. All were rescued, except for a young boy who died entangled in the ship's rigging. Many successful rescues were carried out over the years by the lifeboat crew, which included the pilots. When the Athena wrecked a mile north of Llanddwyn in 1852, attempt to rescue by rowing the lifeboat around the southern tip of the island proved futile. The lifeboatmen enlisted a team of horses to pull their boat over the dunes for a closer launch, saving 14 men. Sadly, four pilots and two apprentices were drowned in January 1874, while attempting to take a pilot off the schooner, Margaret, in a strong wind. The capsized pilot boat came ashore at Dinas Dinlle, near Caernarfon. The older, shorter beacon became an automatic lighthouse in 1972 when the light was transferred from the taller tower. On the rocks offshore cormorants may be seen drying their wings. The small sheep seen in the fields are Soay sheep, an ancient breed. From the tip of the island, there are spectacular views across Caernarfon Bay to the hills of Lleyn *(Llyn)* and Snowdonia.

6. The walls of this cottage have been buried for several centuries. The largest room was the living room. It probably had an open hearth, and near this there would be a raised platform where the family slept. Animals may have been kept in the smaller room. This is probably one of the houses of Rhosyr village which, according to local tradition, is buried under the sand.

7. The southern area of the sand dunes, Newborough Warren, is a nature reserve well known for its wild flowers. Powdered shells make up a high proportion of the sand, making it rich in lime. A wide range of orchids grow here, including helleborine. Oystercatchers, lapwing, curlew, skylark and meadow pipit breed in the reserve.

Walk Directions: (-) denotes Point of Interest

1. Starting from the car park, near the crossroads in Newborough (1), turn right along the lane. Pass St Peter's Church and continue to a left bend. On the right, archaelogical excavation has revealed the foundations of a medieval court (2).

2. Return along the lane 100 metres to a track beside the church. Follow it and take an enclosed path on the left behind the churchyard. Continue through kissing-gates and emerge in a large field.

3. Cross the field ahead to a stile and gate at the edge of the forest (3). Follow the clear path and in about 100 metres take the right fork.

4. Continue through the forest and keep ahead at all junctions. In about 1½ miles the track reaches a small parking area above the beach.

5. Take the track on the right and either follow it to the beach or shortly bear right on a narrow path through the pines. It passes a clearing before emerging on the beach.

6. Follow the beach to the right and take a path across *(Ynys)* Llanddwyn Island. Note – at high tide the island may be cut off for an hour or two. Reach the ruined church (4).

7. Continue to the pilots' cottages (5) and the lighthouse.

8. Make your way back to the beach and bear right. In just under a mile reach a track leading to a car park and toilets.

9. A diversion can be made here to the site of a medieval house. From the car park bear left to follow red topped posts. Pass a picnic area and turn right on a track with the red symbol. The house is about 150 metres ahead, below a hill (6).

10. Return to the beach and continue to the end of the forest. Take a path into the dunes. Continue on a clear path with the forest on the left and dunes on the right.

11. Beyond the end of the forest, pass a ruin on the right. In about another 150 metres, at a kissing-gate on the right into the nature reserve (7), turn left on a green track.

12. The track becomes metalled. Pass the entrance to Maes-y-

Ceirchdir on the right. In about another 40 metres turn right on a track at a kissing-gate.

13. Follow the track as it bends right. Go in front of the house to a kissing-gate.

14. Follow the left edge of the field to the next kissing-gate. Continue with gorse and rocky outcrops on the left. Keeping some distance from a house on the left, follow an old fence. Cross a stone stile beside a gate.

15. Turn left on a track. At the lane turn right to the starting point at the car park.

Facilities:

Large car park (charge) at the end of the lane, near the beach. Toilets at the car parks. Refreshments in Newborough. Camp sites nearby. During the summer months, an exhibition and some period rooms are open to the public in two of the pilots' cottages. Short waymarked trails start from the forest car park. Model village on the A4080 near Newborough.

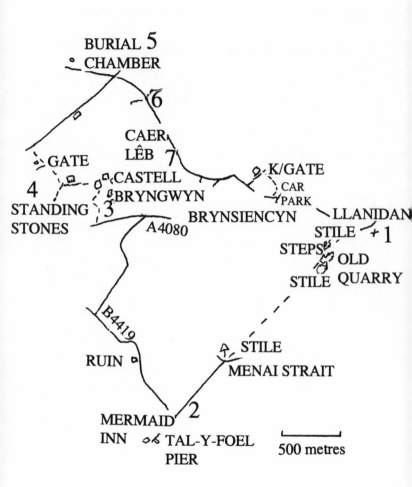

Brynsiencyn – Llanidan – Menai Strait (Afon Menai) – Castell Bryn Gwyn – Bodowyr – Caer Lêb – Brynsiencyn

OS Maps:	1:50 000 Landranger Sheet 114; 1:25 000 Pathfinder Sheet 768.
Start:	Brynsiencyn car park, at the crossroads on the east side of the village, G.R. 484671.
Access:	From Menai Bridge (Porthaethwy) take the A4080 to Brynsiencyn. Buses from Bangor and Llangefni.
Parking:	Brynsiencyn car park.
Grade:	Strenuous – field paths, tracks, lanes and road.
Time:	5 hours.

Points of Interest:

1. Llanidan medieval church was abandoned and partly demolished in 1844 when a new church was built in Brynsiencyn. At present it is closed for restoration but the 15th century arcade can be seen from the gate. An Augustian community was here before the Dissolution of the Monasteries.

2. Before Telford built his suspension bridge over the Menai Strait, ferries were the only means of travelling from Anglesey to the mainland. The Tal-y-foel ferry carried passengers from the old pier here to Caernarfon until late July 1954. Several accidents have happened to ferries in the Strait and during 1723 the Tal-y-foel ferry capsized and almost everybody drowned. A boy survived by holding the tail of a horse which swam ashore, while one man hung on to the boat until rescued. The first known accident – and the biggest – happened in 1664 when passengers were ready to leave the ferryboat at Abermenai Point. The oars had been put away when an argument

arose between the ferryman and a passenger over a penny increase on the fare. Unnoticed by anyone, the boat drifted away from the shore and then, possibly due to panic, capsized drowning nearly all the passengers. Only one man managed to swim ashore. Many local people believed the disaster was a form of divine vengeance because the boat had been built with timber from the disused church on Ynys Llanddwyn. Perhaps the most tragic accident of all happened in 1785 when passengers were late returning to their ferry in Caernarfon. It left with 55 persons on board about one hour before low water. Strong winds made it impossible to keep the boat in mid-channel and it drifted onto a sandbank. Attempts to refloat the boat failed and it filled with water forcing the passengers out of the boat. Their cries for help were heard and boats came out to help, but could not get close enough to save them. All drowned with the exception of one man. By making an improvised raft with an oar and the boat's mast, and after struggling in the icy water for two hours, he finally reached the shore near the Tal-y-foel ferry house. His name was Hugh Williams and he lived at Aberffraw. Another ferry disaster happened in August 1820 when the ferryman, whilst untangling the sail, fell into the Strait. Passengers trying to help him capsized the boat and nearly all the people on board drowned. Again, one man survived – by holding on to the mast until rescued. His name was Hugh Williams and his home was near Llanidan.

3. Castell Bryn Gwyn dates from the late Neolithic period, although it is now quite different from the original earthwork. Excavation in 1959-60 revealed late Neolithic flints and pottery under the bank. The first earthwork was surrounded by a ditch and it is thought possible that the site may have been a henge. (A henge is a ceremonial area enclosed by an earthwork and ditch.) Later the banking was moved and enlarged several times, with new ditches. Pottery of the 1st century AD was found in the enclosure suggesting occupation in the Roman period and the final reconstruction of the defences took place about that time.

4. The two huge Bronze Age standing stones are separated by a gate. The taller one is 4 metres high, the other is 3 metres. It is possible that

originally there were more stones and these two may have formed part of a circle. At one time a small cottage was joined to the thinner stone.

5. The Bodowyr burial chamber was erected in the Neolithic period and its capstone stands tall resting on three stones. The chamber was originally approached by a passage on the eastern side and the whole monument had a covering of earth and stones. The site has not been excavated.

6. On the south bank of the Afon Braint, to the left, two or more hut circles may be seen in the corner of the field. Agricultural improvements in the 19th century destroyed a large settlement which stretched about 500 metres east along the river. Some Roman coins were found when the huts were destroyed.

7. The Iron Age settlement of Caer Lêb is surrounded by bankings and ditches with an entrance on the east. Excavation in the 19th century found the base of a hut circle and signs of rectangular buildings. Finds included pottery of the 2nd-4th centuries, indicating occupation during the Roman period.

Walk Directions: (-) denotes Point of Interest

1. Starting from the car park, turn right along the lane towards the Menai Strait. Pass a wood and reach a stile opposite a track to a farm. Continue on the lane 150 metres to view the ruins of Llanidan church (1).

2. Return to the stile and bear slightly right across the field to the far right corner where there is a marker post and stone steps in the wall.

3. Bear left then quickly right on a path through the trees and undergrowth of a disused quarry. Pass a marker post. At a more open area, keep close to trees on the left to reach a stone stile.

4. Follow the left edge of two fields and cross the middle of the following fields to reach a narrow gate. Aim for the left-hand wall and a stone stile to the left of trees.

5. Turn right on the beach and follow it to the lane. Bird watching can be rewarding here, along the Menai Strait, especially in the winter when waders are present. Continue on the lane to where a road joins from the right.

6. Turn right now or, preferably, keep ahead to visit the Mermaid Inn by the old Tal-y-foel pier (2). Retrace your steps from the inn and follow the road inland.

7. Pass a ruined cottage on a left bend and continue another 600 metres to a narrow lane on the right. Follow it to the main road, the A4080.

8. Turn left, downhill, and in 400 metres turn right on the track for Castell Bryn Gwyn. Follow it to the gate giving access to the enclosure (3).

9. Leave the earthwork by a large ladder stile. Slant left towards a house and cross a corner stile. Keep ahead then turn right through a gate. Cross a stile on the left and another next to it. Follow the left boundary to a field gate on the left at two standing stones (4).

10. Retrace your steps to the corner of the field and turn left to follow the right-hand wall. Cross a ladder stile and keep ahead through a gate to cross a bridge. Pass a pool on the left and keep ahead to a lane.

11. Bear right to a junction. Turn left for 600 metres to a kissing-gate on the right giving access to the Bodowyr burial chamber (5).

12. Return to the junction and keep ahead on the lane almost opposite, passing a cottage on the right. Cross a little bridge (Pont Sarn Las) over the Afon Braint (6).

13. Continue ahead and ignore a footpath sign on the right. In a few more paces reach a kissing-gate and Cadw sign for Caer Lêb (7).

14. Continue on the lane and take the left fork to the road. Turn left and follow the road where it bends right. In another 200 metres turn left on a track.

15. Pass a house on the left and turn right through a kissing-gate. Follow the right boundary of the fields to a stone stile.

16. Turn right then left between buildings to the road in Brynsiencyn. Turn left to the crossroads and the start.

Facilities:

Toilets at the car park. Refreshments at the Mermaid Inn and Foel

Farm (animals and cafe). Sea Zoo. Pick your own fruit farm near Brynsiencyn. Plas Newydd a National Trust property is 3 miles from Brynsiencyn, off the A4080. Burial chambers at Plas Newydd and north of the A4080 there is the well known Bryn Celli Ddu monument. Camp site at Brynsiencyn.

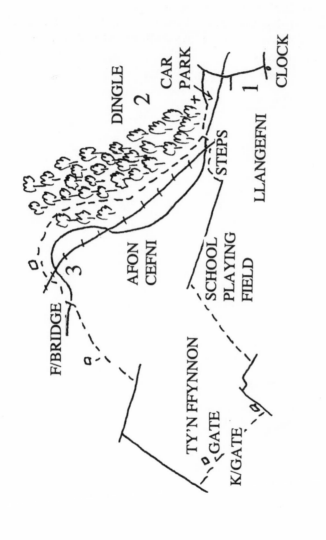

CLOCK

1

LLANGEFNI

CAR
PARK

DINGLE

2

STEPS

AFON
CEFNI

SCHOOL
PLAYING
FIELD

F/BRIDGE

3

TY'N FFYNNON
GATE

K/GATE

500 metres

Llangefni – Y Dingle – Afon Cefni – Llangefni

OS Maps:	1:50 000 Landranger Sheet 114; 1:25 000 Pathfinder Sheet 751.
Start:	Llangefni Town Hall, G.R. 459757.
Access:	From Menai Bridge (Porthaethwy) take the B5420 to Llangefni. Alternatively, take the A5 and leave it on the A5114. Buses from Bangor, Holyhead and Amlwch.
Parking:	Llangefni town car park.
Grade:	Easy – woodland, riverside and field paths, road.
Time:	2 hours.

Points of Interest:

1. Until about 200 years ago the Afon Cefni was navigable to Llangefni. Lying two miles off the A5, this small, inland, market town is the administrative capital of the island. On Thursdays there is a busy market when a large number of colourful stalls fill The Square. The Methodist John Elias preached here in the 19th century.

2. Y Dingle is one of the few woodlands on Anglesey with public access. The footpath winds through mature oak and beech woods following the Afon Cefni and an old railway line. Look out for woodland birds such as the treecreeper, nuthatch and stock dove. Dippers may be seen on the river.

3. At present closed, the Anglesey Central Railway line, from Gaerwen to Amlwch, is a standard gauge line, 17½ miles long. The line was completed in 1867 and there were stations at Gaerwen, Holland Arms, Llangefni, Llangwyllog, Llannerch-y-medd, Rhos-goch and Amlwch. An extension was made to the Octel chemical works on the coast north of Amlwch in 1952. The full passenger journey took 40 minutes and in 1939 six trains ran every Saturday. Beeching closed the line to passenger traffic in 1964 but the Octel works continued to use the line

for freight until they switched to road transport for their products. A preservation company is hoping to reopen the line using steam locomotives.

Walk Directions: (-) denotes Point of Interest

1. Starting from the clock, near Llangefni town hall (1), cross the road and walk along Church Street and bend right to cross a bridge.

2. Turn left at a parking sign and pass St Cyngar's Church on the right. Continue on a path into Y Dingle (2) and pass a footbridge across the Afon Cefni.

3. Ignore a broad path on the right and continue on a clear path through the woods to emerge in a field.

4. Keep ahead and pass a ruin on the right. Cross a ladder stile and go under the railway (3). Cross a stile and shortly a footbridge over the river.

5. Go directly uphill. Do not go through the kissing-gate ahead but bear right and follow the fence through a gap into the next field. Keep ahead and cross a rough stile in the corner.

6. Join a track on a bend. Keep ahead to the road and turn right.

7. Take the first lane left. In 300 metres turn left on a drive to Ty'n Ffynnon. Keep ahead through a gate into a field.

8. Keep ahead to a kissing-gate in the right corner. Continue by the left edge of fields and follow a drive to a road and turn left.

9. In 100 metres turn right and shortly bear left into a housing estate. Reach a T junction and turn right passing bungalows.

10. In about 70 metres turn left on an enclosed path. It emerges in a school playing field. Follow the left edge to the road.

11. Turn right and continue past the Leisure Centre. Pass the entrance to Coleg Menai and turn left at a footpath signpost. Descend a long flight of steps to the river.

12. Follow the path under the railway bridge and cross the footbridge over the Afon Cefni. Turn right and retrace your steps past the church to the start in Llangefni.

Facilities:

Alternative parking near the church. Toilets close to the town car park. Full facilities in Llangefni. Exhibitions at Oriel Ynys Môn. Bird watching at Llyn Cefni.

WALKS WITH HISTORY

Circular Walks in the Brecon Beacons National Park

TOM HUTTON

WALKS WITH HISTORY

Circular Walks in Gwent

RICHARD SALE

WALKS WITH HISTORY

Circular Walks in Gower

NICK JENKINS

Walks with History

Walks on the Llŷn Peninsula
PART 1 - SOUTH & WEST – N. Burras & J. Stiff.
ISBN 0-86381-343-7; **£4.50**
This series combines walks with history, stories and legends. Pastoral walks as well as coastal & mountain panoramas.

Walks on the Llŷn Peninsula
PART 2 - NORTH & EAST – N. Burras & J. Stiff.
ISBN 0-86381-365-8: **£4.50**

Walks in the Snowdonia Mountains
– Don Hinson. 45 walks, mostly circular, 96 pages, inc. accurate maps and drawings. 96pp ISBN 0-86381-385-2; New Edition: **£3.75**

Walks in North Snowdonia
– Don Hinson. 100km of paths to help those wishing to explore the area further.
96pp ISBN 0-86381-386-0; New Edition; **£3.75**

New Walks in Snowdonia
– Don Hinson. 43 circular walks together with many variations. This book introduces you to lesser known paths and places which guide book writers seem to have neglected. Maps with every walk. Pen & ink drawings.
96pp ISBN 0-86381-390-9; New Edition; **£3.75**

Circular Walks in North Pembrokeshire
– Paul Williams, 14 walks, 112 pages. ISBN 0-86381-420-4; **£4.50**

Circular Walks in South Pembrokeshire
– Paul Williams, 14 walks, 120 pages. ISBN 0-86381-421-2; **£4.50**

From Mountain Tops to Valley Floors
Salter & Worral. ISBN 0-86381-430-1; **£4.50**
Detailed information for casual/family walks and for the more adventurous walker.

NEW FOR 1998:
Circular Walks in the Brecon Beacons National Park;
ISBN 0-86381-476-X; **£4.50**
Circular Walks on Anglesey; ISBN 0-86381-478-6; **£4.50**
Circular Walks in Gower; ISBN 0-86381-479-4; **£4.50**
Circular Walks in Central Wales; ISBN 0-86381-480-8; **£4.50**
Circular Walks in Gwent; ISBN 0-86381-477-8; **£4.50**

Mountaineering & Botany

The Complete Guide to Snowdon/Yr Wyddfa
– Robert Joes. PVC Cover; ISBN 0-86381-222-8; **£6.95**

The Lakes of Eryri
– Geraint Roberts. Wildlife, fishing and folklore enhances this book aimed at anyone who loves Snowdonia. PVC cover; 256 pp; ISBN 0-86381-338-0; **£8.90**

The Mountain Walker's Guide to Wales
– Colin Adams. A comprehensive guide to 100 routes covering 200 Welsh peaks. 192 pp; ISBN 0-86381-154-X; Map, PVC Cover; **£6.90**

The Botanists and Guides of Snowdonia
– Dewi Jones. An account of the local guides and the plant hunters. 172 pp; ISBN 0-86381-383-6; **£6.95**

Travellers in Wales

Visitor's Delight
– Dewi Roberts. An anthology of visitor's impressions of North Wales. 152 pp; ISBN 0-86381-224-4; **£3.75**

The A-Z of Betws-y-coed
– Donald Shaw. Full of facts, stories and history about the popular Welsh resort. 136 pp; 0-86381-153-1; **£2.99**

Snowdonia, A Historical Anthology
– David Kirk. 60 writers portray the people and landscape of one of the most beautiful regions in Europe. 248 pp; ISBN 0-86381-270-8; **£5.95**

All the Days were Glorious
– Gwyn Neale. George Gissing in North Wales – quotes from Gissing's letters and diary. 56 pp; ISBN 0-86381-286-4; **£2.95**

The Land of Old Renown – George Borrow in Wales
– Dewi Roberts. A retrace of George Borrow's journey through Wales. ISBN 0-86381-436-0; **£4.50**

Both Sides of the Border
An Anthology of writing on the Welsh Border Region by Dewi Roberts. ISBN 0-86381-461-1; **£4.75**

A Tour in Wales by Thomas Pennant
An old classic abridged by David Kirk. 176 pp; ISBN 0-86381-473-5; **£5.75**

Revd John Parker's Tour of Wales and its Churches (1798-1860)
Abridged by Edgar W. Parry. ISBN 0-86381-481-6; **£4.75**

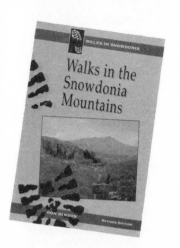

WALKS IN SNOWDONIA

Walks in the
Snowdonia
Mountains

DON HINSON

REVISED EDITION

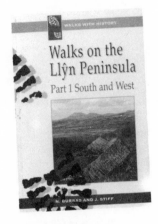

WALKS WITH HISTORY

Walks on the
Llŷn Peninsula
Part 1 South and West

N. BURRAS AND J. STIFF

NEW WALKS IN GWYNEDD

From Mountain
Tops to Valley
Floors

DAVE SALTER & DAVE WORRALL

Aviation in Wales

Early Aviation in North Wales
– Roy Sloan. From early nineteenth century balloon flights to the outbreak of World War II. 168 pp; ISBN 0-86381-119-1; **£2.75**

Wings of War over Gwynedd
– Roy Sloan. Aviation in Gwynedd during World War II.
200 pp; ISBN 0-86381-189-2; **£4.50**

Aircraft Crashes in Gwynedd
– Roy Sloan. Flying accidents in Gwynedd 1910-1990.
168 pp; ISBN 0-86381-281-3; **£5.50**

Down in Wales
– Terence R. Hill. Visits to some war-time air crash sites.
94 quarto pp; ISBN 0-86381-283-X; **£6.50**

Down in Wales 2
– Terence R. Hill. More visits to air crash sites. ISBN 0-86381-401-8; **£6.95**

Welsh History

Donald Gregory's Series – Guides to historical locations with a brief history:

Wales Before 1066 – A Guide
144 pp; ISBN 0-86381-396-8; maps/illustrations; **£4.00**

Wales Before 1536 – A Guide
160 pp; ISBN 0-86381-250-3; maps/illustrations; **£4.50**

Wales After 1536 – A Guide
156 pp; ISBN 0-86381-318-6; maps/illustrations; **£4.95**

The Battles of Wales
– Dilys Gater. An account of battles on Welsh soil.
128 pp; ISBN 0-86381-178-7; **£3.00**

Historic Shipwrecks of Wales
– Dilys Gater. 136 pp; ISBN 0-86381-216-3; **£3.50**

The Young Republicans
– 'Gweriniaethwr'. A record of the Welsh Republican Movement.
184 pp; ISBN 0-86381-362-3; **£7.50**

The Day Before Yesterday
– Donald Gregory. Historical essays on the living past.
ISBN 0-86381-371-4; **£4.50**